CW00860292

To Hull & Back

Short Story Anthology 2014

INTRODUCTION

Welcome to the first (hopefully of many) To Hull & Back short story anthologies. I hope you enjoy feasting your eyeballs on this delightful collection of stories and that the imaginative nature of the tales makes your brain explode.

Hmm. Well, maybe not explode. That might be painful. And messy. I hope the stories enlighten your brain with wonderment. That's probably more appropriate...

The collection starts with the three winning stories, followed by the three highly commended tales from the runners-up in alphabetical order (based on story title). After that, you will be able to read the other 14 shortlisted stories, again, in alphabetical order.

Then, to close the anthology, there is a story written by each of the judges. This isn't so they can show off. It's so future entrants to the competition can see the types of stories the judges write and learn about their tastes. Considering this should give writers a better chance of penning a successful entry for next year's competition.

As a final note, I'd like to express my gratitude to all the authors of the stories that appear in this anthology. It's been a pleasure reading them all and it's an honour to be able to present them in this collection.

Chris Fielden

CONTENTS

JUDGE'S STORIES

ACKNOWLEDGEMENTS

Thank you to Carrie Breeze, Christie Cluett, Josh Keeling, Leah Eades, Mel Ciavucco and Steph Minns for helping me judge the competition. Our writing group website is www.stokescroftwriters.com

Thanks to Elisabetta Bruno for designing the fantabulous cover of this book – you can learn more about her artistic amazingness at www.thinkcreation.net

Thanks to David Fielden for building and maintaining my website and making sure I don't destroy it with updates – without his help, the competition would not have been possible to run. You can learn more about his website building talents at www.bluetree.co.uk

Thanks to Georgie Fielden, Mark Fielden and Mary Fielden for their help with proofreading this book and Georgie for her assistance in filming the To Bath & Back example video, which you can see on my website, www.christopherfielden.com

And finally, a BIG thank you to everyone who entered the contest. There were a multitude of truly amazing stories entered into the 2014 competition and I wish I could have awarded every one a prize. Sadly, I'm not rich.

i

WINNING STORIES

HOW NOT TO UNDERTAKE AN EFFECTIVE TIME-AND-MOTION STUDY

The winning story, by Mike Scott Thomson

1. Closely examine the tasks in hand

To secure an internship at the prestigious, blue-chip, FTSE 100 company, Cresswell Associates, was a rare opportunity indeed. Therefore, when the offer of an interview came through, Gareth Tompkins was delighted. However, the surprise was to be told it would take place at nine o'clock in the morning. On a Sunday.

"Sunday, you say?" he'd enquired down the line to Sir Maximilian Cresswell's PA.

"You heard correct," affirmed the PA, her infinite reserves of patience manifest in her weary voice. "Consider it to be…" she'd paused, mulling over her words, "…your first test of character."

Sounded fair enough; and certainly in keeping with the formidable reputation of this famously fickle, workaholic multimillionaire. The fact this Knight of the Realm was to conduct the interview himself was testament to that.

All in all, for Gareth Tompkins (BBA (Hons), MBA) it was a chance too good to ignore – and the big day was approaching fast. So, all he would be required to do was attend Cresswell Associates at nine o'clock the following morning, switch on the charm, and dazzle Sir Max with his prowess in the specialist field of Business Change.

Surely the post would be his. It was precisely what he deserved. After all, he'd graduated with a First from Fortingdale University, and with his thesis 'Who's Been Counting the Bean Counters?' singled out for special commendation (a hefty tome chock-a-block with Gantt Charts and Boston Boxes), it was difficult to see what could go wrong.

2. Spot opportunities to be more efficient

At any rate, it would beat his current employment at the local Pop-In-For-A-Pizza. Gareth, emitting his customary stench of sun-dried tomatoes and dough after yet another gruelling shift, glanced at his wristwatch. It was 12 minutes to 11, almost time to knock off. As per usual, he'd single-handedly finished the closing time tasks with superhuman rapidity. So, as

2

the customers drifted away, he'd topped-and-tailed the seats, from the perimeter of the room inwards, averaging a saving of 20 seconds per table. With 30 tables in total, that accounted for 10 of these 12 spare minutes. One further minute was saved cleaning the surfaces (his approach was to wipe-as-you-go, donning a money belt stuffed with several pouches of fresh J-cloths, avoiding the faff of frequent return visits to the storeroom). The final spare minute came from Gareth dispatching the last of the perplexed diners much faster than what might be considered standard, even for a fast food joint. Having adapted the restaurant's portable Chip 'n' PIN machines to double as Pez Dispensers (your bill and after dinner mints in one go), he'd saved an extra 30 seconds per table without resorting to another fruitless wrestle with those stubborn plastic sweet packets. (Such struggles inevitably led to frantic scrambles for the establishment's sole pair of pinking shears, which were there for no other reason than it was the one tool capable for performing this otherwise Herculean task.)

Yes, Gareth thought, *Cresswell's was somewhere he could* really *put his skills to good use.*

He glanced at his watch again. 11 minutes to 11. So: 13 minutes to cycle home, seven minutes to prepare for bed, four minutes to arrange his suit for the interview, and, with it taking 35 minutes to cycle from his bedsit to Cresswell Associates on the other side of the city, he'd have a decent eight-hour sleep before awaking refreshed and raring to go.

From behind him he heard a cough. It was Bryan, the restaurant owner. "Still here, Gareth?" he said.

"Yeah," Gareth said. "Done everything I needed to, so..."

Bryan shrugged; the morose resignation of a manager who, in every aspect of his business imaginable, had been trumped by this precocious young upstart. (In an unprecedented act of self-demotion, he had even begun to undertake the home pizza deliveries himself on the company motorbike, rather than delegate this thankless task – anything to get away from the constant feeling of being second best in his own business.) Puffing his cheeks, he glowered at Gareth. "You may as well go now, then."

"Cheers, Bryan," said Gareth, making for the door.

"Oh, and Gareth?"

Gareth stopped and turned towards his current, hopefully soon to be ex, boss.

"Remember, the clocks change tonight."

Gareth swallowed the tiniest of dry gulps. "Yeah, thanks," he said, trying to pretend he hadn't forgotten. "See you tomorrow evening," he said, exiting the restaurant to the bike rack.

How, he thought to himself, had that small fact eluded him? He allowed himself a rueful chuckle. Was it that time of year already? The nights had been drawing in, all right. Of course, his iPhone would update automatically. Only his wristwatch needed doing. Holding the silver button on the side of the clock face, the minute hand rotated steadily until it pointed to its new position of eight minutes to 12. Gareth made some adjustments in his head as he did so. Fine, he thought. No biggie. Seven hours sleep instead of eight would still be all right. Still adequate time to shower, dress and breakfast too.

He unlocked his bike, swung his leg over and perched himself on the seat. At once something felt odd. He was tilting backwards. He turned to look at the rear wheel.

A flat. Blast.

He levered himself off again, cursed under his breath, and began the half-hour walk to his bedsit, his bike clack-clacking along beside him.

3. Make operational changes in order to achieve them

It had been a deep and dreamless sleep, and Gareth slumbered into the early hours of Sunday morning with all the peace and tranquillity of somebody whose alarm has failed to go off. By virtue of a slowly sprouting sapling of doubt creeping up from his subconscious, he did, eventually, awake. As his eyes flickered open, he thought to himself, *strange.*

Bleary-eyed, he reached for his wristwatch. The upside-down smile of an 8:20 grimaced back at him.

In years to come Gareth would look back at the ensuing five minutes with a mixture of admiration and incredulity. How *did* he spring himself out of bed and gallop to the bathroom (two and a half seconds), piss (an agonisingly long and frustrating 42 seconds), wash (a hopelessly inadequate 38 seconds), wrestle himself into his suit (two minutes), stuff his iPhone, keys and 'Who's Been Counting the Bean Counters?' into his satchel (three seconds), put on his shoes (two seconds; luckily they were slip-ons) and propel himself out the front door and into the cool, dark autumn morning (half a second)?

Yet at the time, the methodology behind his truncated morning routine was not foremost in his mind. Instead, his vocabulary, spoken through clenched-teeth whispers to nobody other than himself, consisted of nothing more than some colourful and inventive swearing, with the occasional inclusion of, "What the bottoming arse happened to the alarm on my arseing iPhone?"

Outside, the uncombed and hyperventilating Gareth once more looked at his wristwatch. 8:25. 35 minutes to cycle to Cresswell's. Perfect. But...

His bike. The flat tyre. Double blast.

In contrast to the havoc of the previous five minutes, Gareth took the next 10 seconds to stand stock-still and think. So: it was a Sunday morning. There were no trains running, at least not to where he needed to be. Buses were sporadic at the best of times. Could he call a taxi? It would take at least half an hour for one to turn up. So then, no. Wincing, he looked down at his legs, both of which were trembling, seemingly sapient at the prospect of what they'd shortly be made to do.

With a shudder of disbelief and determination, Gareth sprang forward, sprinting down the deserted avenue towards the city centre.

4. Prepare to take calculated risks

Despite this unscheduled burst of cardiovascular activity, Gareth couldn't help notice how quiet the streets around him were. It might have been a Sunday morning, but there should have been *some* traffic about. Yet in 15 minutes of continuous running, as he tore down the road with leaping strides, only one car, a silver Mercedes, passed by. Instinctively he stuck out his thumb – since when had he ever hitched a lift? – but when the car failed to slow, speeding off in the very direction he needed to travel, he switched his hand signal to one with a somewhat different message. "Arse bucket!" Gareth shouted, his hoarse voice echoing down the silent street. Groaning to himself, he continued to run.

By the time he breathlessly reached Pop-In-For-A-Pizza, he knew it was hopeless. Already it was quarter-to, and he wasn't even halfway there. This golden opportunity, the one he'd been waiting for and wanted above all others, was slipping from his grasp. Repeatedly kicking himself wouldn't begin to atone for this idiocy.

There was no way he'd make it now. Unless...

The restaurant. The motorbike. He'd ridden it before, doing their deliveries on a provisional licence, before his stealth takeover of the shop floor. If he could remember how...

Gareth bolted across the road, down the alley and round the back. There the machine stood in the pre-dawn twilight, battered and scratched from its incalculable journeys. It should get him there in time. Just.

He swung his satchel off his back, unzipped it and fumbled for his large bunch of keys. In the course of his efficiency drives, Gareth had seen fit to get multiple copies cut of every key the premises used. Now this foresight had paid off. Kicking the bike stand away, he hefted himself onto the seat, forced the helmet onto his sweaty head, clipped off the longest and thinnest key he found on the bunch, and inserted it into the ignition. There followed a sequence, but what was it? He clasped his eyes shut in concentration. *Choke. Turn key. Kill switch. Start button. And...*

A loud splutter sounded from the engine, followed by the rumble of some healthy revving. He laughed – a triumphant outburst over the din – and, swinging the bike around, he was back on the road, leaving the suburbs 10 times faster than his poor legs had been able to carry him.

5. Determine whether this produces the expected results

As Gareth roared up to the glass-fronted building in the heart of the financial district, he had brief visions of himself somersaulting over the handlebars through the double doors to make an inappropriately acrobatic entrance. Fortunately, he recalled how to brake just in time. As he disembarked next to an oddly familiar silver car, he discovered he'd forgotten to re-zip his satchel and the copy of his thesis had, somewhere en route, vanished.

He shrugged. To hell with his thesis. It was two minutes to nine; the important thing was he'd actually made it. Smoothing his jacket, he strode through the double doors and into the lobby.

After being directed to the office at the end of the nearest corridor – "There's always one," muttered the bored receptionist, cryptically – Gareth paused for breath, knocked twice, and, on the dot of the hour, entered.

Behind an oaken desk, in the otherwise empty room, sat the silver-haired, Italian-suited figure of Sir Maximilian Cresswell. The palm of his left hand propped up his head. His left elbow, in turn, rested on the desk.

"Zzzz," said Sir Max.

Gareth stood there, for once unsure. So much for the 'workaholic' Sir Max. Remembering what the PA told him on the phone, he assumed that deciding how best to proceed, subsequent to actually turning up at this ungodly hour, would be his next test of character.

Gareth raised his fist to his mouth and gave two short coughs.

The reaction from the multimillionaire was like a string puppet being yanked to life. Sir Max's arm shot down, his head tilted upwards, and two eyelids flipped open to reveal penetrating blue eyes. Bewildered, he blinked, quickly glanced at his Rolex, then focused on the young man standing in front of him.

"And you are?" barked Sir Max, now unnervingly alert.

"Gareth Tompkins," said Gareth Tompkins.

The older man's face creased with barely concealed disbelief. After a second or two, he relaxed, leaned back in his chair, and raised his eyebrows in what appeared to be acceptance. "There's always one," he said, echoing the receptionist's words from moments before. "That's why I do these things," he continued. "This time of morning. This time of year. Catch 'em out. Roots out the deadwood, you know? But you, Tompkins," he said, leaning forward again, "you take the proverbial biscuit."

"Excuse me?"

"I said, take a seat."

Gareth did so.

"First question," said Sir Max, a wave of distaste flitting over his lined face. "Is it a habit of yours to attend important business conferences reeking of..." he sniffed, "dough, and..." he sniffed again, "... tomatoes?"

Gareth had to confess it wasn't.

"Second question," went on Sir Max. "Is it *customary* for a prospective employee to address their would-be employer as, and I quote, an 'arse bucket'?"

Gareth also had to confess it wasn't. He gulped. His throat was very dry indeed.

Sir Max frowned and sat back in his executive chair.

"Final question," he said, raising his eyes to look at the now less-than-confident Gareth. "This is also a straight yes/no question, but take your time nonetheless." The multimillionaire squinted. "You put your clocks *forward* instead of *back* last night, didn't you?"

Gareth responded with neither yes nor no. However, a merry ditty, proclaiming, "Wake up, it's a beautiful morning!", emanating from his vibrating iPhone at its pre-programmed moment of 7:05, answered for him.

6. Rinse and repeat

As an ashen-faced Gareth steered the misappropriated motorbike through the alley to the restaurant's yard, blood further drained from his face when he spotted his boss, loitering in the open air, biding his time. Indeed, this newly-empowered Bryan, having turned up merely to oversee the weekend delivery, now had all the reason he needed. And, from the looks of what he was holding, evidence too.

Gareth switched off the engine, removed his helmet, disembarked and sighed.

Bryan also sighed, but one of relief. With decisiveness, he thrust out a slightly rained-on copy of a time economics thesis.

Gareth retrieved his paperwork, and handed over the motorbike key and helmet.

The two men eyeballed each other.

Bryan jerked his head in the direction of the high street.

Gareth, with no need to ask what this wordless exchange signified, mooched away.

Back out on the high street, his ego irreparably wounded, he passed a green recycling bank. He stopped, looked at the bank, then regarded the tome of meaningless drivel he still held in his hand. Without thinking, he posted it through the slot. It hit the bottom with a hollow 'bong'.

So, that was that, then.

From his satchel came another vibration. He retrieved the device and looked at the screen.

A call.

"Sir Max wished to make it known that time is essentially an artificial construct," were the first words the PA said from down the line.

"Pardon?" said Gareth.

"In other words – he's decided he likes you."

The PA took Gareth's silence to be a gigantic question mark.

"It transpires," she explained, "that you passed a test of character, of sorts. Sir Max has never in all his years witnessed anyone in quite so much of a hurry to meet him." She paused. "I couldn't possibly imagine why."

"So..." Gareth ventured.

"You start nine o'clock. Tomorrow. Oh, and Mr Tompkins?"

"Yes?"

"The very best of luck. You *will* need it."

Gareth thanked the PA, and hung up.

He stood motionless on the street corner, phone in one hand, satchel in the other. A fine drizzle peppered the air.

OK, thought Gareth. And then, as an afterthought, *that's nice.* But he remained where he stood; then stayed there some more. Long enough, in fact, to lose all sense of time.

And as he looked to the gradually lightening skies, it

dawned on Gareth that he had, after all, got precisely what he deserved.

~

Mike Scott Thomson's Biography

Mike Scott Thomson's short stories have been published by a number of journals and anthologies, including *The Fiction Desk*, *Litro*, *Prole*, *The Momaya Annual Review*, and *Stories for Homes* (in aid of the housing charity Shelter). 'Me, Robot', his story to feature in *The Fiction Desk* anthology *Crying Just Like Anybody*, was also adapted for performance by the theatre group Berko Speakeasy. Competition successes include the runner up prizes in both the *InkTears* short story competition (2012) and the *Writers' Village* international short fiction competition (2013).

Born in Essex and raised in Sussex, he now lives in the part of Greater London which somehow has a Surrey postcode. For a day job, he works in broadcasting.

Mike's website: www.mikescottthomson.com

~

Mike Scott-Thomson – Winner's Interview

1. What is the most interesting thing that's ever happened to you?

When I was a teenager, I was a very keen magician. By far the youngest member of my local Magic Circle, I would often perform stage shows, or baffle audiences with my ever-present pack of playing cards. On one occasion, I performed on stage with none other than Paul Daniels and the 'lovely' Debbie McGee (note to non-UK readers: Paul and his assistant wife Debbie were the two most famous television magicians of the 70s and 80s). As a young conjurer, I had the privilege of sawing Ms McGee into not merely halves, but three pieces. That, to be sure, was an interesting experience.

Whilst I no longer perform magic, I often see parallels between performing magic tricks and writing fiction. Both, in their different ways, are forms of storytelling, creating an imagined possibility out of nothing. Both use misdirection, hiding the obvious in plain sight. Over two decades later, my teenage wizardry has probably shaped me as an author more than I realise.

2. Who is the most inspirational person you've ever met and why?

That's a very difficult one to answer. I couldn't single anyone out as most inspirational, since many people I meet inspire me in different ways.

I can give one example. Almost ten years ago I quit my job to spend three months living in Düsseldorf, where I took German lessons at a local institute. I was making slow progress; I could only understand the gist of what was being said, or worse, nothing at all. Then one week, our new teacher, Frau Föllmer her name was, breezed in. She had no lesson plan. Gone was all the boring grammar and dry textbooks. Instead she spent every lesson sitting on her desk, yammering away in very quick German, talking the hind legs of a donkey. Initially, all the students were baffled. *Crikey*, we thought. *Slow down*.

But as the days went on, and as she engaged the class in proper, stimulating conversation rather than throw endless verb tables and case declension charts our way, we began to find every word she spoke seeped into our brains. Finally, it all made perfect sense.

I'm still not sure whether this was because of what she said, or if it was the way she said it; but to me, the important thing was that it was engaging and entertaining. It's something I've remembered ever since.

3. Which authors do you most admire and why?

David Mitchell: staggering breadth of imagination, with some very funny writing thrown in; I'm especially thinking of the segment 'The Ghastly Ordeal of Timothy Cavendish' from *Cloud Atlas*.

Philip K Dick: best science fiction writer ever. I have a whole bookshelf devoted to him.

Michael Marshall Smith: his *Only Forward* is the first book I think of whenever I'm made to think of an all-time favourite.

I also very much admire Terry Pratchett; I'm slowly working through all his *Discworlds*. He's not just a great fantasy author, or a great comic novelist, but a great writer full stop.

4. When and why did you start writing short stories?

On a few occasions, I've tried to write novels – but never finished one. There's a good reason: I tend to have a gut instinct if what I'm doing isn't working out.

It was obvious I needed practice writing. I also

needed a sense of accomplishment, namely, to actually finish something I started. One week in late 2011, my writing group challenged its members to write romantic comedies, so I decided to have a go at writing a quick tale. The result went on to be published and win a couple of prizes. Somehow, where I hadn't been able to pull off a novel, I found I had an aptitude for shorter fiction.

I don't see short stories as any way inferior to novels; they're different forms, with different challenges. However, I have always found them a much better prospect for experimentation and practice. To my mind, it's far better to spend a week or two on a bad short story and learn from the experience, than plough away for months on end on a flawed novel.

Sooner rather than later, I will attempt a novel again. When I do, I will see it as a sideways move (not 'graduating') from the short story; I can't see a time when I'll ever not write them.

5. Where do your ideas and inspiration come from?

Often, the seeds of my ideas are planted from brief observances: a news story, an image, an overheard conversation. A few times, however, I stumble upon a topic ripe for lampooning and I simply cannot resist. 'How Not to Undertake an Effective Time and Motion Study' was inspired by an occasion in my day job where I had to express the time I spent on all my responsibilities as a fraction of a percentage, type them into a grid which contained 14 different colours, save it as a CSV file and upload it to a shared drive, the URL of which contained a dollar sign, a wiggly squiggle and a pair of square brackets. If you've understood any of that, then you've done better than I did.

My story was therefore an attempt to untangle that particular conundrum (and I still see a certain glory in its pointlessness), and although I clearly didn't succeed in that respect, I'm pleased my story took on a life of its own. Short fiction very often does that; they begin with one thing in mind, then turn out to be a completely different creature.

6. Where do you write?

I have a study in my flat where I do some writing, but not as much as I should; very often I find the walls start to close in. As a result, I'm prone to taking my iPad and keyboard to a selection of local cafés, and spending an hour or two there. Occasionally I go to the London 'Write Together' groups on Meetup.com. Some writers don't find the busy atmosphere in cafés conducive to creativity, but I find the soft hubbub and general lack of distraction quite helpful.

7. How do you cope when your writing is rejected?

I've always been OK with it. Certainly there've been occasions where I've particularly admired a literary journal or competition and would have loved to be included. Failures to be accepted into those have inevitably led to disappointment.

But you do have to see the positives. If a work of mine has been rejected multiple times, there's probably something not right with it. In those cases I will either try to re-write it, or junk it altogether, chalking it up to experience. (Besides, do I really want a piece of my work for all to read which is not as good as it possibly could be? The honest answer is, no. Best, therefore, to regard rejection in these cases as a blessing.)

Often, though, a story will be turned down by an editor or judge, simply because it doesn't meet their taste, or the editorial requirements of the publication. Again, I chalk that up to experience, and remember what those tastes and prejudices are for future reference. You learn more from failures than successes.

8. Who has published your work before?

I've been fortunate enough to have had my work included in some very fine publications, including two anthologies from *The Fiction Desk*, literary magazines such as *Litro* and *Prole*, and a book of short fiction in aid of Shelter, *Stories for Homes*. I've also come runner up or been shortlisted in a few competitions, including *InkTears*, *Writers' Village*, *Momaya Press* and *Writers' Forum*, but have never achieved a first place. Until now!

9. Why did you choose to enter the To Hull & Back competition?

This one is easy: because I wanted to support it. There seems to be so few opportunities specifically for humorous writing; in fact, I can only think of one other award for comic literature, and that's for published novels, not short stories.

I wonder why this is. I don't think it's because the literary world in general lacks a sense of humour. So many times I've read judges' summing up notes in competitions, or editorials, bemoaning the lack of humour in their submissions, or saying what a relief it is to come across a good, funny piece of writing amidst the solemn, serious stuff. Yet despite this, very little comic fiction seems to be published.

I therefore think it's great Chris started this competition, and so many wonderful writers entered. Long may it continue.

10. What will you spend your prize money on?

Books. I'm out of shelf space though, so I suppose I'd need a new bookcase as well. Then I'd need an additional wall for this new bookcase to prop up against. But there's no room in my flat for another wall, so I'd better go house hunting...

Can I start again?

EBooks. I'll buy some eBooks.

11. What has been your proudest writing moment so far?

I would definitely include coming first in the 'To Hull and Back' short story competition. It's my first outright win, and I'm obviously very proud.

In addition, one of my stories, another comic piece entitled 'Me, Robot', was read aloud at the Berko Speakeasy, a short story cabaret. Their actor dressed the part of my narrator, donning a spray-painted outfit and coating his face with silver. Witnessing a story of mine literally come to life was another very gratifying moment.

12. What advice would you give to novice writers?

There's a good quote from the literary critic and writer Cyril Connolly: "Better to write for yourself and have no public, than to write for the public and have no self."

The measure of a successful writer, I guess, is when they get to the stage they do both – both write something they really want to write, and have lots of people want to read it – but it's a good maxim with which to get going. So, if you're just starting out, I'm with Cyril: don't write for anybody other than yourself. Tell the tale you want to tell, and tell the tale that only you can.

Also remember that first drafts are rarely very good. The important thing is you crack on with it, finish that unpolished gem of a first draft, and have fun whilst doing so. The result is much more likely to be entertaining and engaging.

Edits, re-writes, targeting your work towards potential markets, publication... these all come later. To begin with, just concentrate on telling that story. That's what I have to continually tell myself, anyway.

PSYCHO

The second place story, by Christopher Berry

I was looking forward to moving. To no longer having to stare at the same four walls. It was exciting. And when I was excited, I always dreamed of happy things. A glittering trough of golden grain, topped with moist blackberries, and crispy grasshoppers on the side.

But on the night before the move, there wasn't even a hint of a grasshopper leg behind my eyes. Instead, those *things* were back again. Those *things* that had recently been taunting me in my dreams. Every time I went to sleep, the same series of strange images returned to stalk me.

Firstly there was a padlock. A big, metal padlock, attached to a wooden hatch, kept flashing in front of my eyes. And for some reason the sight of it brought me out in a sweat.

Why? I've seen lots of padlocks in my life. They're just chunks of metal – they never bothered me before.

But *this* padlock frightened me. It made my wings tremble and my wattle throb.

Then something else formed in the black hole of my sleep. A white square. Moving towards me. There was a thick, red 'L' in the white square, which made me dizzy and want to throw up.

And a pair of orange scissors. They just appeared – in the depths of my periphery. Floating towards the white square with the bold, red 'L'. The scissors opened like a mouth, swooped across the white square, and sliced the 'L' in two.

And as it did, I could hear a dog. Nasty vermin. It was barking, growling very near me. I could feel the drool it spat from its juddering jowls against my feathers. I could hear its paws rapping the ground, getting louder, as if it was running towards me.

And finally, the chug of a rickety train rumbled through my ears, and an urgent whistle startled me awake.

It wasn't the first time I had dreamed of these things. Dreamed of the 'L', the orange scissors, the dog, the train...

The next morning, Farmer George welcomed us all into our new pen. After my somewhat turbulent night, I was calm and content again, looking forward to spending some time with my fellow turkeys within the new walls.

But when George left, and he attached a padlock to the hatch to keep us in, that was when it all changed.

As I looked at the padlock, a deep feeling of dread spiralled up my long neck, like I was regurgitating a very long worm.

No. The padlock. The padlock from my dreams.

"Ron, are you OK?" asked Jezebelle, the lady I was hoping to mate with in the spring.

I didn't answer. Scraping my talons through the straw, scratching the concrete beneath, I prepared to charge. Then I did, and with all of my might I slammed my body into the hatch and broke through it. The padlock snapped off the hatch and spun to the ground.

I crept into the pig pen. The pigs were fast asleep and silent as usual, but for the occasional rumbling of flatulence. I swept past the pigs, quietly flapped my wings and lifted myself over their gate, into the sheep pen.

I slinked into the shadow behind a trough of water, my snood wobbling with adrenaline, as Farmer George came back in with a pair of orange scissors.

Orange scissors.

"Come on, Samuel," said George to one of the sheep. "We left you with a very 80s quiff after your last shearing. We can't have that."

"Noooooo!" I let out a shrill holler in turkey-speak, and stampeded towards the farmer's legs.

Startled, George dropped the scissors, which plunged towards his left foot, sliced through his old, flimsy boot, and severed his toe.

I dove to pick up the scissors, gripping them in my beak, blood dripping from the blades. With George having left the gate to the sheep pen open, I was able to make my escape. I spun out of the barn into the cow field.

"Beatrice, where's that turkey going with those scissors?" I heard one cow say to another.

"God only knows, Doris," muttered the second cow.

"I told you this would happen, didn't I? The programme is wrong!" I could hear Farmer George's yells as I flapped my wings over the fence enclosing the cow field. He must have been shouting at someone on his mobile phone.

I landed in the road. I had no idea what I was doing. Suddenly, some furious rage propelled me.

I almost calmed down for a second.

What next?

But then I saw a car stop at a set of traffic lights, a few yards down the road. And stamped on the back of the car was the same white square from my dream. With the bold, red 'L' in it. Suddenly my bitter fury was reignited, and like a bullet I charged at the vehicle.

"Right. At the end of this road, I want you to do an emergency stop," said a voice inside the car, as I sneaked around to the front.

The two humans inside let out high-pitched screams when I leapt onto the bonnet, threateningly waving my bloody scissors at them.

"Is that a – is that a *turkey*?" cried the driver.

"It's a turkey with scissors! Drive! Drive!" the older man shouted, making frenzied hand gestures.

But I wasn't budging. I knew what I had to do.

I was going to cut off their ears.

Then an engine roared, a tyre screeched, and I was hurtled off the bonnet as the driver swerved the car. Furiously clambering to my feet, I tried to chase the evil-doers. My efforts were in vain. The humans sped off into the distance, the car's spinning tyres kicking up a mushroom-shaped cloud of dust, dirt and litter that came rushing at me.

The *Daily Farmer* newspaper was blown into my face. I let the pages flutter to my feet, and looked down at the big, black words stretched across the newspaper's centre page, which immediately seized my attention.

Controversy as the Brain Recycling Programme (BRP) is to start using the brains of dangerous criminals.

My snood wobbled with fear as I read the story....

The science team who have developed the process of brain recycling as a way of breeding better livestock have met with opposition. This is after the brain of a psychopath was used in the creation of a rafter of turkeys. Campaigners are now saying – bring back cloning!

The psychopath in question was Ron Slapper, who went mad one day after his wife decided to padlock him in his shed as a joke. When he escaped, he flew into a rage. He took the scissors she was using to cut flowers and cut off her ear. He then stormed out of the house with the scissors. As he crossed the street, a learner driver almost ran him over, and had to slam on his brakes. This infuriated Ron, and he lurched into the driver's window, grabbed the learner, and cut off his ear too.

It was at this point that an old lady across the street, watching the bloodbath, decided to take action. She set her dog on Ron, and the dog, barking fiercely, chased Ron down the street.

The dog chased Ron to the railway track, at which point Ron tripped and fell onto the track. The driver of the oncoming train wasn't able to stop in time and Ron was sliced in half.

Ron's brain, which was still intact, was donated by his wife to the BRP. But it has caused a number of farmers some serious problems...

I was about to read what had happened to several other turkeys across the country, when I heard the sound of another rumbling engine, rolling like thunder towards me.

The screech of brakes pulsed through my ears.

Before I could react, the mammoth wheels of a vast lorry rolled over me. And I was a pancake.

The next day, I made the headlines. I'm reading the *Daily Turkey Heaven* now, as I sit on my little cloud.

Psychotic turkey goes on a scissor rampage. The proof that officials need to stop the brain recycling.

Fancy that. I'm a turkey and I've helped to make a difference in the world.

Go me.

~

Christopher Berry's Biography

Christopher Berry is an author and copywriter currently residing in Hampshire, England. He has published a number of children's books, including a fantasy novel, *The Pendulum Swings*, and a series of illustrated books for children, *The East Pudding Chronicles*. These are stories about the 'alternative' origins of Christmas traditions, such as mistletoe, crackers and Christmas trees, in the vein of Roald Dahl and Tim Burton's darker manner of storytelling. All these books are available on Amazon.

Christopher is currently working on a trilogy of

novels called *Million Eyes*, featuring some of Britain's most famous unsolved mysteries, cover-ups and conspiracy theories - with some time travel thrown in for good measure. He will soon be submitting the first book to agents and publishers. He also runs a blog called *Behind The Curtain*, a lighthearted look at some of the world's biggest mysteries and conspiracies.

Chris's website: www.crberryauthor.wordpress.com

THE BISCUIT BURGLAR

The third place story, by Adele Smith

I was born into the wrong family. Not that I would express this opinion openly. That would be far too dangerous. My family was different from most others. We had a family business that was unconventional and definitely not one most would want to inherit. No one earned a pay cheque, not because we were rich or lazy. We lived on our wits. We were professional thieves.

I was not born to be a thief. I was born to bake.

I started baking after our mum died. I was 14 years old when I first picked up a whisk. No one else seemed to know what the kitchen was for. So, whilst Dad was busy turning his grief into anger and my brothers were toughening their outer carapaces, I dusted off the recipe books and began to cook. Cakes, cookies, pastries, pies, plaits, pretzels, macaroons, muffins, flapjacks, biscuits, nothing was too challenging for me. I worked my way through cookbooks like my dad and brothers did car manuals.

As the food began to appear on the table, no one said a word. Not even thank you. I should have hung an 'Under New Management' notice over the kitchen door because they treated it like a café, just as they had when Mum was alive. Perhaps cooking was my way of coping, sublimating my grief.

That was how it started.

Being a member of the Brash clan, stealing was not a choice, it was expected. I began marking jobs not by hit rates, but by the allocation of my baked goods. I was incapable of going to a job empty handed. It was a lesson our mother had taught us.

"Never go to someone's house without a gift." I took her at her word. No one knew what I was doing, at least, not for quite a while.

Driving to a job, if anyone said, "Can anyone smell baking in this van?"

I would say, "Yes! It's just something I made for afterwards. In case we get hungry."

"You're an 'eadcase, Rob, you know that, don't you?" This was my younger brother. He called everyone an 'eadcase, even though it was a term best suited to him.

What I didn't tell them was that I always brought something extra. Something for us and something for the owners of the house we were about to break; a round of shortbread, a dozen chocolate chip cookies; it was my way of saying sorry.

We were good at our job. True professionals. Everyone knew their role and played it well. Brad, the eldest, he was the driver. He sat in the van whilst we went in. Dad and Trent, the youngest and man most likely to run the business after Dad, they were the real deal – the thieves with the lightest fingers. They did the selecting and the bagging up. My job was look out. I would watch for the occupant's return. Some thieves leave a bottle or a broom on the door handle, something that they can hear if the targets come back unexpectedly. I am a far more efficient early warning system. I spot them the minute that they turn into the drive. Every extra second counts in our game.

Dad and Trent never stay in the kitchen, not after they've checked for house keys and handbags. There's never much worth taking in the kitchen. So, when they were upstairs or in the other rooms, that's when I went to the kitchen with my baked offerings. Today I was leaving shortbread. Everyone likes shortbread. Last week it was muffins, the week before that, gingerbread. I was worried about the gingerbread. I worried that it might have made some people even angrier. Ginger was peppery. Not everyone is partial to ginger. I wanted them to feel at least a little compensated for the loss of their valuables.

I got the idea of making labels after I saw one of our hits on an episode of *Crimewatch*. Our jobs had been on before but they'd never caught us, they never even came close. They interviewed the 'victims' as they always refer to them, or worse, 'innocent victims of opportunist thieves'. That annoyed me. One thing we were not was opportunists. Everything was carefully planned. So, *Crimewatch* were in the kitchen, interviewing the householders, as I prefer to call them, and I noticed my calico bag of biscuits still there on the table. They hadn't even seen them! This upset me. I had left them on the kitchen table in plain view. For them! Talk about a lack of gratitude! After that, I made sure each gift was labeled. In block letters, it said:

DEAR OCCUPANTS, PLEASE ACCEPT A GIFT OF HOMEMADE [INSERT NAME OF BAKED GOODS]. APOLOGIES FOR THE LOSS OF YOUR PERSONAL ITEMS.

Now there would be no doubt over my gift and its intention.

I began to see a recipe in everything. I made one about our work: 11 easy steps to housebreaking. It went like this:

For this burglary, you will need the following:
- *One pair of gloves*
- *One torch*
- *Dark-coloured clothing*
- *Assorted tools: Crowbar, screwdriver or mallet (according to taste)*
- *Two/three towels or tea towels (to muffle sound and wipe surfaces)*
- *Two/three suitcases (you will find these inside the house, usually in the bedroom or box room, but have own set aside as backup)*
- *One broom or glass bottle (to place on the door handle)*
- *Optional extra: front/back door key if available (try under doormat or plant pot)*

Method:
1. *Select your scene: pre-check the area you intend to visit. Choose your dwelling carefully, based on one or more of the following: high fences or hedges, no other buildings overlooking property, an open or broken gate, single door lock, lack of*

security doors or a 'beware of the dog' sign ('beware of dog' sign = no house alarm)

2. *Once you have made your selection, ensure your targets are out of the house*
3. *Sift out the most vulnerable point of entry*
4. *If necessary, apply gloves or crowbar to disable security lights*
5. *Gain entry. This may require using tools, but if optional extra is available, add to keyhole now*
6. *In a separate location, ensure the driver is standing by*
7. *Add broom or glass bottle to door handle to allow for early warning of a likely disturbance*
8. *Using your gloves, gather up as many items as possible. Note: do this quickly to ensure a smooth finish. Use torch as required*
9. *Fold selected items carefully into suitcases and ensure the latches are well secured*
10. *Exit building as rapidly as possible, adding all ingredients to get-away vehicle*
11. *Leave scene to cool off for at least 10 days*

That was the recipe we followed if all went to plan. Simplified, of course. But there were times when it was not so simple. Even the best in the business can make mistakes. This is the story of our last robbery. Nothing about it followed our family recipe.

First, our van wouldn't start.

"What's wrong wiv the bleedin' fing?" This was Dad addressing Brad.

"Bloody 'ell, Dad, 'ow should I know?"

"Well you're the bleedin' mechanic of the family."

"Yeah, Dad, a mechanic, not a bleedin' magician!"

"Biscuit anyone?" I said. A biscuit with a cup of tea could solve anything in my mind. It was me who got the van to start. I don't know how. Whilst everyone was eating my shortbread and sipping tea, I turned the key in the ignition and it fired.

"Perhaps you're not such an 'eadcase after all," said Trent.

"Well done, son." I think that was the most praise my dad had ever given me. It didn't last long.

This job was my responsibility. I had cased out the house last week in the guise of a salesman but as usual, my heart wasn't in it. I missed things, important details. I was too busy thinking about the shortbread I was going to bake later.

As soon as we arrived I sensed that something was awry but not wanting to tarnish the good impression I had made on Dad with the van, I kept my mouth shut. Besides, it would be OK. I had my labeled shortbread biscuits tucked firmly in my jacket.

The front door of the house had a security grille. I didn't remember that from my earlier visit.

"I fought you said this was an easy entry?" said Dad, speaking through his balaclava.

I shrugged away my self-doubt and not wanting to lose face, I said, "We have to enter round the back. It's much safer and we're not overlooked." This seemed to appease my father and brother, but the sweat had already started to trickle down my cheek. It was only when we jumped the fence that I really started to worry. There was a dog, a small one, but with a very big bark, which it was now employing.

"There's a bleedin' mutt!" Dad was really angry now. He cocked his head to one side, which only meant one thing: he was sizing you up for a punch in the face. I liked small dogs, unlike my dad and brothers who preferred the larger, more solid arm and leg-removing breeds.

"Silence it!" spat Trent. Dad and Trent both looked at me. This was my job and it was up to me to fix it. My hands closed round the biscuits in my pocket. It was lucky I had thought to bring two batches. Breaking the shortbread triangles into pieces, I threw them down for the little Jack Russell, who immediately scoffed them. I doubted that shortbread was ideal for dogs, but what happened then was a surprise. The dog fell on its side and started snoring. At least it was quieter than barking.

"'Ave you killed it wiv your bloody biscuits?" asked Dad.

"No, I think he's...well, he's..."

"What?"

"He's in a...sugar coma? They do have rather a lot of sugar." Dad pushed at the dog with his foot.

"I don't care as long as he ain't barking. Let's just get inside and get this over wiv." I made a mental note to adjust the sugar in the recipe for the next batch.

The backdoor was an easy access. I got one thing right. There was no security door and the lock was easy to jimmy. That was lucky because I knew I had led them to the wrong house. I wasn't about to admit it, though.

We were in. Dad and Trent sprang into action and went upstairs. On the way up, Dad checked again.

"Son, you definitely checked this place out, didn't you? No surprises on the calendar or anyfing?"

"Course, Dad!" I lied. I was in too deep to change things now.

"Good. Well, keep an eye, then."

"I will." I knew Dad didn't really believe me. Trent was already upstairs, trashing his way through someone's irreplaceable treasures. He didn't care. He just wanted what he could sell. He was keener than me, keener than Dad or Brad too. Trent had a drug habit to feed. Dad appeared at the head of the stairs.

"Rob! Where're the suitcases? You said you'd done this place! Where the 'ell are they?"

"Err...not in the wardrobe?" I hedged. Dad was spitting through his teeth in his lowered voice.

"No! Try again. Where did you see them?" I was starting to panic now. I wondered if honesty might not be the best policy.

"Umm...well, I think I may have missed them."

"So, what you're saying is, there aren't any and you never bovered to point this out."

I swallowed hard. "Well, I..."

"Trent!" Dad cut me off, not interested in what I had to say. "Stop looking." Dad turned his glittering eyes on me. "You! Get the bloody bags from the van. Now!" There was no point arguing with Dad. You just did as you were told. On my way back through the kitchen, I glanced around with my torch. It was instinctive. You always check your immediate surroundings for changes. The torchlight brushed over the kitchen calendar. If this had been the house we were supposed to be in now, the one I had *actually* scouted out, this would have been the first thing I would have checked. All the houses in this area looked similar. Big and flashy.

I found today's date. There was something written there: '12 Angry Men 8pm Mercury Theatre'. I wasn't exactly from a household of thespians but even I could work out that tonight, our targets were at a show. I checked my watch. It was 11.30pm. How long did plays go for? It was then that I heard the sound of a car pulling up. Two seconds later, my phone began to vibrate and the following three things happened simultaneously:

1. Dad yelled my name, followed by a string of unrepeatable swear words
2. Brad appeared at the kitchen window and started doing a vigorous mime, the gist of which appeared to be that the targets had just arrived home
3. I heard the unmistakable sound of footsteps on the driveway followed by a key turning in a lock

There was only one thing left for me to do. As the unwitting occupants entered their dwelling and flicked on the hallway light, I fixed my brightest smile.

"Surprise!" I yelled. "You have been selected for *The Baker's Dozen*, a new TV show which asks members of the public to taste test a range of homemade products and give their verdict live on TV." I was banking on shock as the smokescreen to cover the fact that I had let myself into their home and there was no TV camera crew. Everyone liked being chosen, didn't they? I hoped that this would give Dad and Trent enough time to get out of the house.

"We've been what?" said a bewildered middle-aged man, blinking at me in the harsh hallway light. I sharpened my smile.

"Selected as contestants for a new TV show!" Everyone wanted to be on the TV, didn't they? "All you have to do is try my homemade shortbread! Close your eyes and open wide!" Too surprised to argue, the middle-aged man and his presumed wife closed their eyes and allowed me to shove a shortbread triangle into their mouths. Luckily for me, shocked faces tended to lend themselves to open mouths quite naturally. Before their brains had time to register the strangeness of this situation, I had sprinted through the front door behind Dad and Trent and was back in the van.

Dad removed his balaclava and turned to me.

"Rob, tell me again how you checked out that place?" I knew this was not a general enquiry about process. There was nothing for it. I knew I had to come clean. Trent saved me the trouble.

"It was the wrong bleedin' house, wasn't it? Say it!" Trent was at his most dangerous when his voice was calm.

"It was the wrong bleeding house," I repeated. "Sorry."

When the tabloids coined the phrase 'The Biscuit Burglar' I knew I was in trouble. Of course, the family knew it was me. They weren't stupid.

"Biscuits? 'Ave you gone soft in the 'ead or somefing?" said Dad.

"You're an 'eadcase!" said Trent.

"It was just a little acknowledgement. For our trouble. What's the harm?"

"What's the 'arm? What's the 'arm? DNA! Yours! All over the bloody biscuits!" The vein in Dad's head was bulging so I knew he was properly angry.

"I wear surgical gloves," I reassured them. Dad's vein was about to pop.

"How long's this been going on?"

"Biscuits and cakes! At every job! 'Ave you lost the plot?" said Brad.

"You're an 'eadcase," said Trent, never one to vary his phrasing.

For the first time in our criminal history, the Brash clan was jittery. We laid low. Naturally, they allowed me to shoulder the blame for the fact that we were now the laughing stock of the entire criminal underworld.

It didn't stop me baking. Neither did it stop my family from wolfing down my baked creations.

I saw the TV news. A middle-aged man was speaking to the camera, being interviewed outside a house I recognised.

"I know we were victims of an attempted robbery, but the quality of the shortbread was amazing! I would really like the thief who made this to get in touch."

Get in touch? I could barely believe my ears. It was a terrible risk, though. It could be a police trap. On the other hand, we didn't actually take anything from his house. I was tired of being a thief and he really liked my shortbread...

"Come in! Rob, is it? I just wanted to tell you in person. You are a wonderful baker. The shortbread we sampled simply melted in the mouth. It's the reason I wanted to meet you. I was wondering, are you working at the moment?"

"Well, no, sir, not exactly. Sorry, I don't know your name."

"It's Arthur," said the middle-aged man. "Arthur Kipling."

I was born into the wrong family. Not that I would express this opinion openly. That would be far too dangerous. My family was different from most others, but perhaps not so different anymore. Brad was training to be a mechanic, Trent had gone back to college to do a Diploma in Applied Science with a chemistry specialism and Dad had retired. For the first time in his life, he could relax. No one made the vein in his head pop out any longer. Everyone was happy, doing what he enjoyed.

Me? Thanks to Arthur, I began my traineeship as a baker and now, I bake for one of the biggest companies in the world. But my shortbread recipe, that, I will take with me to the grave.

~

Adele Smith's Biography

Up until four years ago, I was a full-time teacher of drama, so for me, writing was born more from a sense of panic than gradual self-realisation as I sought to bail out the least prepared of my GCSE students with my hastily scribbled monologues. After sixteen years in the job, I decided that my days of being the back-up writer were over. It was time to try it alone.

Since leaving full-time teaching in 2010, I have completed three novels: *The Garden Dancer*, *Left Field* and *Show Me Where*. I have also written twelve short stories, three of which received commendations or long-list mentions in competitions. 'The Biscuit Burglar' received third place in the *Lady in the Loft* competition last year. Alas, the publishing deal still eludes me but I intend to keep working on that, even if it takes me the rest of my life.

Now I work as a fitness instructor and sometimes teacher and write to please myself, as long as it fits around boxing classes and boot camps, hoping for the day when I can give it all up and do what I enjoy most in the world: writing.

HIGHLY COMMENDED STORIES

A MEETING OF THE MINDS

Highly commended story, by Kathryn England

The Picklings lived in a weatherboard shack a stone's throw from the sea. As both were octogenarians well and truly set in their ways, the pair agreed on little. But one afternoon, due to fault on both sides, they found themselves on the same wavelength. The day had started like most in that the two had kept out of each other's way. It helped that each Pickling had a little patch of garden in which to potter. 81 year-old Sam grew the juiciest peaches that had ever graced the branches of a fruit tree. 80 year-old Alex grew the sweetest strawberries that had ever dangled from a stem. Neither shared their bounty with the other.

But there were times when a peach grower's mouth watered at the thought of strawberries and cream. That morning, when Alex had ducked out to buy some tobacco, Sam had ducked out to the garden to pick six plump strawberries hidden under leaves. Unknown to Sam, Alex had already picked two ripe peaches on the blind side of a branch to eat on the walk to and from town.

When Alex got back, Sushi was waiting inside the gate. Overfed on fish and love, Sushi was a large cat. As Alex bent down to pick her up, the front door creaked open and something shot out in a blur of fur and teeth and zeroed in on Sushi like a heat-seeking missile.

"You did that on purpose," Alex accused when Sam stepped onto the porch, eyes rolled skywards. "You saw me comin' and you let 'im out!"

"I never," Sam replied indignantly as Benny, a short-haired terrier, chased Sushi up a tree. "I was just coming outside to soak up some rays. Anyway, my dog's doing that moggie a favour, giving it some exercise. You shouldn't feed it so much. It waddles round like a pint-sized brontosaurus. It'll have a heart attack one day. And Benny's not only giving it exercise, he's teaching it to be wary. You don't want it thinking dogs are playmates, do you? It's got to have a healthy fear of canines, otherwise it might try to play with that Doberman down the road and get its head ripped off."

Alex gave Sam a look that could have frozen a buzzard in mid-air then went over to the tree and tried to coax Sushi down from a branch. "I've told you a million times she ain't an it, she's a she. And I heard what you said to that fleabag of yours. You said, 'Sic 'im, Benny.'"

"You need your ears tested," Sam said. "What I said was, 'Must ring Lenny.' You misunderstanding me is like a story I heard once about this soldier who passed a message down the line that said, 'The general wants reinforcements, he's going to advance.' Well, the message got repeated over and over and by the time it got to the last soldier he was told, 'The general wants three and four pence, he's going to a dance.'"

Alex's face went as blank as a roll of cheap loo paper. "I dunno what you're goin' on about but you don't know no Lenny."

"How d'you know who I know and who I don't know? Met Lenny last week at the shops. Hit it off right away. Promised to give him a call one day."

"Pull the other one."

Sushi scrambled into Alex's outstretched arms and the pair went inside.

Sam sat on the porch long enough to make Benny's accidental escape seem plausible then went to have a lie down in one of two bedrooms that stood side by side at the rear of the house. On finding Sushi curled on the pillow – a trifle unusual because the cat always slept in Alex's room – Sam plucked her from sleep and dumped her unceremoniously outside the door where Rex was waiting to help her run off some more pounds.

So, half of Sam and Alex's day had passed in the usual fashion.

After lunch, however, they decided to try to catch a fish dinner, something they did at least once a week. They had fished for a living in their prime and fished for enjoyment in retirement. Both reckoned they had so much sea water in their veins that when their sweat dried they had to chip off the salt. After dragging their wooden rowboat down to the shore, they each took control of an oar. They'd been fishing an hour or so when the boat sprang a leak.

"Don't just sit there," Sam said. "Plug it. If you can't find nothing else, use your finger."

"I'm not sticking me finger in that hole to get it all splintered," Alex said. "You plug it, you stupid peanut. If you'd mended the boat, we wouldn't be sinking."

"I did mend it. But who was it went to the store and got that newfangled stuff that obviously don't work? You should've got black pitch, you ninny."

"Black pitch?" Alex spluttered. "Nobody uses that no more, you silly galoot. I told you that. But as usual, you don't listen."

Sam grabbed their metal bait bucket and tipped the contents over the side of the boat. "Start rowing while I bail!"

Alex's beady eyes sank into their sockets like two raisins in a lump of scone dough. "You row! It's your fault we're here."

"That's what you reckon, is it?" Feeling that the unfairness of the accusation needed a physical response, Sam threw the bucket which bounced off the rim of the boat, landed in the sea and sank.

"Now look what you've done, you twit!" Alex yelled. "How we gonna bail water with no bucket?"

Sam's cheeks glowed. "How d'you figure that everything's my fault? You're the one bought prawns 'stead of pilchards. The tailor would've been running near the breakwall this morning. If we'd gone for them with the pilchards we wouldn't be so far out. But 'cause you got prawns we're stuck out here fishing for bream, ain't we?"

"Well, if you'd fixed the boat proper we wouldn't be sinkin', would we? And what's that eatin' our bait? Sharks?"

Sam glanced sideways – the water was frothing like a school of piranha on a hippo carcass – then stood up, fists raised. "I'm sick of your whinging. I'm gonna knock your block off."

Alex rose to the challenge with fists clenched so tightly they were as drained of blood as a pair of pork knuckles. "You and whose army?"

The two lunged at each other, banged heads and fell backwards into sea water slapping around the bottom of the boat.

"Crikey this water's cold," Alex said. "Me bum feels like a frozen chook."

Sam noticed that one of the boat's wooden slats had come loose from their fall. "We've sprung a bigger leak!"

It was quite obvious that the rim of the boat would soon be at sea level and so would they. Alex grabbed the oars and began to row while Sam used cupped hands to bail. Before they knew it, the oar handles were up around Alex's ears and Sam may as well have been trying to empty a bathtub with a fork. Sitting at either end of the boat they went down with the ship, as far as their necks anyway.

"Well, what now?" Sam said, treading water.

Alex nodded at the shoreline. "We swim."

Fortunately, the two were competent swimmers although neither had attempted such a long swim before. They set off, doing a slow but steady breaststroke. Halfway to shore they rolled onto their backs to take a break.

"You 'right there?" Sam asked, knowing that

smoking rolled ciggies often left Alex breathless.

"Yeah, I'm 'right. You 'right?" Alex asked, knowing Sam's arthritic joints would not be appreciating their unexpected workout.

"Yeah, I'm 'right."

They turned over and continued on. When they reached the shore, they dragged themselves from the water and collapsed onto the sand.

"I've been thinking," Alex said after a few minutes. "On the way to town this morning I saw a little tinny for sale, 500 quid, motor included. We could buy it between us. What d'you think?"

"I think that's a good idea," Sam said. Fishing was the only time she and her sister did anything together.

So, for a while at least, Samantha and Alexandra Pickling had come to a meeting of the minds.

~

Kathryn England's Biography

I'm an Australian and have been writing for about twenty years, mostly for children, but also contribute to magazines, mostly women's fiction. It was actually the magazine fiction that got me started. I received some initial acceptances then got a bit of a head swell and tried my hand at writing children's fiction. I've only recently gone back to the adult fiction because I do enjoy doing both.

LAME DUCK: YOU'RE FIRED

Highly commended story, by Will Haynes

Tuesday evening. I'm just hanging myself. The phone rings.

It's Her. This is awkward.

"I'm busy," I say, "not the best of times. Is it urgent?"

For some reason I still take the call and the obligatory hand-in-hand abuse. Whoever said that it's better to have loved and lost than to never have loved at all was a total chump... She tells me that I'm a fraction of the man she thought I was and to go ahead and think I'm a little Kurt Cobain. It hurts but she's right. I'm simply a lame duck that had been masquerading as a golden eagle and I got found out, or taken out – shot from the sky by cannonball. Bloodied feathers still littered over everything else I see, taste, smell and touch... I couldn't even hang myself particularly successfully. I'm still alive, for a start. All I've managed to do is create a bit of a friction burn around my neck that will take some explaining at work and my throat feels like a silverback gorilla's been pounding on it. I swallow a couple of times to test it out. Maybe not a gorilla... Perhaps a small colobus monkey? I should probably leave a note too. That's the decent thing. Something poetic. Mostly because if I hang myself without one it might look like I did it by accident. One of those wanking experiments gone horribly wrong? Michael Hutchence, sans talent. Just another wannabe wanking himself to death... How embarrassing. I decide not to hang myself. I'll think of something else for another day. To be honest, I'm just quite pleased to have heard from Her at all, regardless of abuse, and so I'm definitely going to sleep on it.

Maybe she still cares?

Week 1

Work again and everyone's talking about that fucking *Apprentice* programme on TV last night. There's general amusement that the guy from it's got the same name as me. I pointed out that it's spelt differently the first few times they cracked the joke but any reaction at all on my part merely encourages further contribution. The mentality at the UK's 6,787th most popular phone-upgrade store is hardly the nation's hotbed of comedic talent. Any talent. Why am I surrounded by cretins? This telephonic boiler room: a clutch of middlemen in the excreting bowels of Service Land, a claustrophobic loft office in Manchester. That's why. Hardly Oxbridge material that end up in this bargain bin at the budget supermarket of last-chance careers. At least this keeps me reasonably secure. I'm Premier Sales Boy here. Scoreboard Champion. Market Leader. King of the Jungle. Of course, I've been cheating but nobody's got the chutzpah to sniff it out. I'm simply hacking in to the re-sales accounts for last year's transactions, rather than cold-calling like we're supposed to be. That's 99% of the battle won, rather than disturbing total strangers with a script – carefully worded so that they wrongly assume you're from their network and it's time for their free upgrade. They will either shout abuse at you, ignore you, hang up immediately, or perhaps if you're very fucking lucky one in 100 might stay on the line, with one in 10 of those that do naively divulging their security details. You then call the network 'on their behalf' and pocket the commission. The ones that go for it are typically the obvious examples: the young, the old, the weak, the sick, the poor, the needy, gullible, desperate and stupid... all of nature's typecast victims. It's not exactly a Ponzi scheme but if they dealt with the network directly they'd get a far superior phone on a much shorter contract. It's hardly what I'd call ethical trading. Sometimes I want to scream, "DON'T FUCKING ACCEPT. HANG UP. NOW. DIAL ONE ON YOUR MOBILE, SPEAK TO YOUR NETWORK IMMEDIATELY AND GET A BETTER DEAL THAN WE COULD EVER OFFER YOU... EVEN IF YOU WERE SIGNING AWAY YOUR SOUL IN YOUR BLOOD, WRITTEN ON THE SKIN OF YOUR FIRST BORN. THIS. IS. NOT. FUCKING. WORTH. IT."

Haven't actually done it yet. Still on my bucket-list if I decide to croak. Make an appointment. Schedule it into the diary. Perhaps tell HR Guy to GO FUCK HIMSELF too.

Awareness of impending death does have its

advantages...

HR Guy comes in and makes the *Apprentice* joke, pointing his finger at me, doing a terrible cockney impersonation before bursting into hysterics. HR Guy: a shrill, lanky creep of a man, a small fish in a tadpole bucket, mercilessly aware that the small power he holds in this stagnant goldfish bowl makes him a 'player' in his tiny, sad world. He resembles an overly libido'd-up skeleton, sporting an 80's flat top in a Primark suit. I sigh inwardly and try to chuckle outwardly, unconvincingly to any sentient being, but satisfied with my response, he moves along to the new attractive Polish girl and makes some comments that in any other company in the First World would end in a cut-and-dry lawsuit with handsome compensation payoff for the recipient. Around here it's merely par-for-the-course. She also chuckles unconvincingly at his hilarious-cum-rape-alarmingly, chilling remarks. I'm not sure which of us HR guy likes more. We're obviously this week's favourites. I bring in more sales, however she is undeniably attractive. And HR Guy thinks he's in with a chance. He thinks I'll make more sales. Either way, we're both safe for now. New Somalian Guy isn't. He's underperforming his targets so he's for the chopping block three days in to his unpaid, legally unjustifiable, grace period. Poor fucker. They'll definitely keep him on until Friday though. I know none of us would do nearly as well as him if we were just getting to grips with our Somalian in a depressing new land of 'opportunity'. We'd have to resort to piracy sooner than he would. Once I've exhausted the re-sales supply I'll be in every bit as much danger as our new Somalian friend. Once Polish has knocked HR Guy back at the first post-work drinks bash, so will she.

This was only supposed to be temporary until the band took off. Somehow it's become a full-time gig, with the band merely a slip-show for the weekends and things. A few small pub 'concerts' here and there. Pocket money if the promoters choose to pay us, which they inevitably don't. I'm 27 now. What did I want to be when I grew up? Kurt Cobain. Jimi Hendrix. Jim Morrison. Janis Joplin? Hmmm... Ian Curtis, maybe? Not him... He was too young. Not actually part of the 27 Club, though he often gets lumped in with them... Where did it all go wrong? For Ian it was topping himself as Joy Division was just on the cusp of superstardom. For me? It started so well: Music Scholarship to Cheetham's. Met my True Love there. Set up a band. Hotly tipped by NME on the 'Ones To Watch' list. Shot a few music videos, one of them in that old condom factory (that is now flashy, overpriced loft apartments that gloat at me from the window of my ex-student digs). A few trips to London. Did some blow. Went nowhere. True Love doesn't love me anymore. She seems to hate me. Now I punch numbers in a hot room. Perhaps it would have been better to go at 22 like Ian and to have been remembered while I still had potential... and She still loved me.

When things are good I hear music all around me. I can compose a symphony from the orchestra of rapping keyboards in the office, soft tones from phones in the background, wind rattling against the windows like percussion. Tubular bells of heavy Manchester rain ringing from potholes in hard concrete streets; sweeping slushes of car-driven puddles, baritone hums of car engines and the rhythmic gudder, gudder, gudder of pneumatic drills splitting tarmac. I even see the noises. I project these resonances from my mind on to passing objects: billboards become musical scroll, objects form shapes of notes, chords and scales: clouds become C-minors, E-flat majors, people appear to be humming backing vocals as they go about their day-to-day business and harmony is all around me... but when it's bad it's very bad... there's nothing. An empty hole, left raw and gaping, a vacuum to be filled only with unfulfilled promise. Music and hope will never return. Today, Polish girl seems to be humming into the phone and I hear a basic melody from some tormented soul scratching nails against the target board. It's not exactly Beethoven, closer to the Sex Pistols, but at least there's something. It's because I've had word from Her that there's at least some form of melody as the score to my life. It's very dangerous to base your entire happiness on another person, but at least I'm not feeling like sucking an exhaust pipe or shotgun barrel right now.

Week 2

There's a movie on. Colin Farrell is being a total bastard to Pocahontas and then he buggers off and ditches her. She's heartbroken. Later on Christian Bale turns up and he's very nice to her. She gets with Christian Bale, forgets Colin Farrell, moves to Buckinghamshire to a big country pile and is happy there, has a few dinner parties with Royalty, and is touted around high society when she visits the West End. Then Farrell turns up again, like the scoundrel that he is, and it screws her up and she gives Christian Bale his marching orders. It's all very close to home but I can't work out if I'm the Farrell character or the Bale one. Or maybe even Pocahontas? I change channel and it's the bloody *Apprentice* again. That cockney geezer with my name is still ranting on about how nobody's going to make a fool out of him, he's been in business 40 years, blah, blah, blah, but he's already making a fool of himself by even considering giving any one of the desperate Muppets that can't even boil an egg a job... I'm pretty sure one of them is a guy who got fired from my boiler room last year. I can imagine HR Guy on it, a talking head by the Thames or some other iconic London landmark, crapping on about how he's in charge of the Premier Sales team in Europe or something and earns squillions but for no apparent reason he wants to jack it in and move to Essex to boil eggs for a questionably applicable 1980's ex-computer salesman...

Haven't heard from Her for over a week now... if love is a drug it's the most dangerous addiction of the fucking lot. Last week's call was like another hit of the hard stuff, Big L, however distorted, and now I'm back to a suffering slow withdrawal of wondering if we'll ever speak again. 'Cold Turkey' is in the post and music is slowly fading out from my world... I've been poring over it all again and again. That look in her eye when I knew it was all fucked plays matinee in the theatre of my mind.

Week 3

Music has stopped entirely. Really should stop watching this bloody show. It's always on Wednesdays that I feel the absolute lowest. Weepy Wednesdays. *Apprentice* Day. I'm not even looking at the TV. I'm on the internet looking up relevant quotes for love and life and death and whatnot – but the volume's up and a cockney accent in the background is screaming, "This is an absolute bladdy disgrace. You lot couldn't boil an egg between ya. An absolute shambles. A bladdy shambles. Ya fired!" Then a bit of a preview about next week's episode and then the theme tune: Dumdum-dum-dum-dum-duuum-dummmmmm... 'Dance of the Knights'. What's the preview of where I'll be this time next week?

Week 4

Sitting on top of Affleck's Palace looking down at a steep drop. Is it 70 floors down from here? Something like that... the grid-like streets below look like the early version of Grand Theft Auto on the Sega Master System, before it got all high-tech and 3D on street level when it evolved to Sony PlayStation. You know, the birds-eye-view one, but the traffic now all looks much smaller than that. People are more like atom-size dots rather than ants... I'll make a hell of a splat. Doubt I'll feel a thing. Haven't written a note. Can't be bothered. No chance of wanking mix-up with this method anyway... Christ, I've always hated heights as much as I have death. Actually, I think I will write a note. I'll go back and watch that bloody programme instead. See who's for the chopping block.

Week 5

Have started the note. It's rubbish. Why did She fire me? WHY!

Week 6

WHY? WHY? WHY? WHY? WHY? WHY?

Week 7

Still haven't written the note. Can't see any musical ones anywhere either... don't want to speak to any of my friends. Not sure if I actually have any. Don't want to watch that fucking programme. Hate Wednesdays so much I've actually decided to work late. I'm the only person in the boiler room. Only sound is a tuneless drone from the overheated fan of this prehistoric desktop piece of shit. I drudge through the re-sales accounts: sold, easy. Sold. Sold. Piece of piss. Sold. Climbing the scoreboard. Sold. Commission earned. Reputation sustained. Sold. Sold. Sold. Kerching. Kerching. Kerching. The sweet sound of minimum-wage commission is the only melody that exists now. I scroll down to the next name on the re-sales list: Mr G. Brennan.

I punch in the digits and a familiar nasal voice floods my earpiece.

"Hello, Mr Brennan?"

"Yes."

"I'm just calling from Top Phones4Me with regards to your Orange mobile phone and I'm pleased to tell you that it's time again for your free upgrade."

"Allen?"

Eh? Alarm bells ring! G. Brennan... Gavin Brennan? It's HR Guy!

"Err..."

"Are you logged in to the re-sales or something?"

Fuuuuuuuuuuuuck! Rumbled.

"Weeeelll... errm..."

It's not like it's a firing offence...

Week 8

Still here... but the old re-sale's password isn't...

Week 9

Work has been harder since they've changed the access code for re-sales. My sales have plummeted, but I'm still selling more than most, though hardly the former lion-status I held in this increasingly threatening jungle. To make matters worse, HR Guy's been even more unbearable than usual since Polish ex-employee knocked him back at Friday's post-work drinks shindig.

I've now tried to call Her a couple of times and they've both been unanswered. The silence is the worst thing of all and I wonder where she is, who she's with and if she's even thinking of me at all. Or if she's simply shacked up in a love nest with her new beau... it's the demotion that kills me the most: a demotion from being the love of her life, potential father of her children, to little more than a social embarrassment, a regret, a stain to be bleached from the bed-sheets of history. In silence I know that I'm permanently fired.

And so to the note I've had my writer's block in regards to composing this past however-long-it's-been... it's in my pocket. It's the best I could muster. It'll have to do. Hardly the perfectly poetic suicide note I'd have liked, but at the end of the day I'm not a writer. I'm a failed musician. I just scribbled it out now after work and so I've not given HR Guy both barrels like I'd wanted. The next life, perhaps... the 19.36 from Stockport should be hurtling through any second now at however many miles an hour. Shouldn't feel a thing.

I hover past the safety line, toes just nudging past

the platform's edge, looking down at the steel track. I'm ready to leave this place. I'm certain that the note will still be legible... it's no great literary loss if it's not. Token gesture. No mix-up of what my intentions, no rumours of experimental masturbation gone wrong at the wake. I doubt there'll be many attendees anyway. Not for a fucking also-ran like me. OK. Ready. Where's the fucking train? Should have been here by now...

What's the time?

Fucking British public transport... so fucking unreliable. Been here for an hour now waiting for the train and still no sign of it.

End up cabbing it home instead and watching *The Apprentice*.

It's the final five.

Week 10

Turns out some guy threw himself onto the tracks at Stockport, which is why the train was delayed. Note in the pocket, the works... for some reason got me thinking and I had an epiphany. Realised we're all going to die one day anyway, so what's the rush? Whether it's good or bad, pretty soon we won't know the difference anyway, so just keep on living. Decided that what I was going to do instead was to keep on living my life and do the things I'd liked to have done and damn the consequences. If they work they work, if they don't they don't, I'll just try my best not to hurt anyone in the process, and the music's quietly creeping back into my life again. Once that happened it got me thinking about everything that happened with Her, and I realised that She didn't fuck it up... I did. All I can think about are all of the good times and good things and do you know what? Sometimes it just doesn't work out, but there's no need to be bitter, no need to wallow in self-pity, and I wish Her nothing but the best. She deserves it. I will always love Her but I realise I'm not right for Her. And I understand what She was trying to tell me, I didn't listen to Her at the time, and I made it all about me, me, me, me. But there's no time for self-flagellation here. I'm going to compose another note...

Week 11

I've put in writing what I now believe the situation to have been, and apologise for my actions. I hope that it helps to heal the raw wounds and Her to be happy. It gives me some inner peace before my next journey too.

I head into the boiler room, posting the letter along the way, and as I arrive HR Guy shoots me the look of a teacher at an errant child that's left a turd on his desk instead of an apple. I'm no longer Premier Sales Boy. Far from it, and the further I plummet on the target board, the higher I'm climbing up his shit list of non-desirables. I couldn't care less. He's leching over a new desirable, an attractive 19-or-so-year-old New Eastern-European Girl, who's not reached the first post-work drinks to test her suitability, in his eyes, for the position.

I'm hitting the cold calls and haven't made one sale yet. Through the office humdrum I make out a faint melody building from the instruments around me, the creaky floor, the tapping of keyboards, the rapping of rain on the windows, the hums of phones, wavering pitches of pleading voices... and it's not a bad tune. I can make something of it. HR Guy is giving New Eastern-European Girl an unwelcome shoulder rub, crapping on about the need for relaxation in the workplace to achieve maximum target sales. The tune takes a darker plunge, stripping back to a deep bass with sharp violin jabs when his claws grip her skin. I'm Googling a number as one of my cold-callees answers: an old lady's trusting voice jingles from the receiver. I deliver the script slowly and very unconvincingly as I'm scribbling down the number, but she doesn't hang up and even though I'm doing my best not to sell the product she still sounds interested. I start going the other way but she seems almost impossible not to sell to, and so I loudly say, "Actually, madam, I've just looked at your details and it appears there's a much better option for you. Whatever you do, DO NOT TAKE THIS DEAL. OR ANY OTHERS LIKE IT... UNLESS IT'S DIRECTLY WITH YOUR NETWORK..."

HR Guy's attention is snapped immediately away from the girl as several more heads in the sweatshop snap from their phoney calls, mostly perplexed, some admiring. The expression on his face is that of a tiger that's just had its prey snatched from its teeth by a housecat, and is currently stunned into inaction.

"...IF YOU DIAL ONE ON YOUR HANDSET NOW AND SPEAK DIRECTLY TO YOUR OWN NETWORK, YOU WILL BE ELIGIBLE FOR A HANDSOME NEW PHONE AND SIGNIFICANTLY CHEAPER TALKPLAN. THIS IS A THIRD PARTY DEALERSHIP, AND NOT YOUR OWN NETWORK, AND WE, LIKE MANY OTHERS THAT WILL TRY TO CONTACT YOU, CAN ONLY OFFER YOU INFERIOR PRODUCTS ON GROSSLY EXTENDED CONTRACTS THAT WILL TIE YOU IN FOR THE BEST PART OF ETERNITY, IN WHAT IS A CASE OF BORDERLINE FRAUD..."

HR Guy's paws are off the new girl, and he's bounding over but I've thanked the lady and have hung up by the time he's at my station. The lanky creep is bearing over me, swinging his pelvis, and the vein above his pulsating eyeballs resembles a knotted hosepipe fit to burst. He's scrabbling, but before he's found the words he's trying so very hard to place, I'm out of my chair. I say, "AND YOU, SIR… ARE A CUNT. I'VE ALWAYS WANTED TO TELL YOU THAT AND NOW I HAVE."

Sweet release. He tries to incredulously spit it out, but it's so stammered, "You're f-f-f–"

"YES. YES. I KNOW, I KNOW. I'M FIRED. GOOD."

I march over to the new girl and hand her the piece of paper I've scribbled on to. I then persist at even greater volume. People in surrounding offices, buildings, towns, villages and countries should be able to hear me.

"THIS IS THE NUMBER OF AN EMPLOYMENT LAW SPECIALIST THAT MAY COME IN HANDY BY THE WEEKEND… IT'S NO WIN, NO FEE, BUT I'M SURE YOU'LL HAVE A SOLID CASE, SHOULD ANYTHING HAPPEN THAT YOU FEEL MAKES YOU UNCOMFORTABLE OR SHOULD YOUR CONTRACT BE TERMINATED UNJUSTIFIABLY. I'M SURE THERE'LL BE PLENTY OF WITNESSES SHOULD YOU NEED TO PURSUE IT, AND A GOOD PLACE TO FIND THEM WOULD BE ANY NUMBER OF COLLEAGUES ON UNPAID GRACE PERIODS WHO WILL BE LET GO AT THE END OF THIS PERIOD. THESE PEOPLE WILL ALSO HAVE VERY STURDY CASES OF THEIR OWN."

I stroll out of the office to a drum roll and the slam of the door behind me is like the dramatic crash of a cymbal. What next? I'm not watching that bloody show tonight. I'm getting the first flight out of here to anywhere in the world. Last chopper out of Saigon. Doesn't matter where… I'm going on holiday to have a think about everything.

Week 12

I'm sitting in a bar on the Kao San Road in Bangkok. It's raining heavily. Tourists' sprint for shelter, the monsoon pelting down like ruddy stair rods. Hawkers continue to tout, unperturbed, beneath fragile but determined paper umbrellas. Drains overflow, as rich aromas of chilli and lemongrass from food-stalls mingle with an undercurrent of sewage from the submersed drainage system. It's bliss. I see a few B-majors bouncing off a fat, wet German man in a wife-beater, and a couple of D-sharps spring along the backpacks of a few fleeting gap-year students, evading the C-minor of a strung-out geriatric hippy as much as they're avoiding getting their MacBook's soaked. I smile at a girl sitting alone on the table next to me, and she smiles back. All the sounds and sights and smells and senses and emotions build together in symphony to form Sergei Prokofiev's 'Dance of the Knights'. I'm thinking *Romeo and Juliet* rather than *The Apprentice*. Music is all around me. Life is all around me.

It's beautiful.

~

Will Haynes' Biography

Will Haynes started his career in the UK film industry as a runner on high-profile feature films, before progressing to various supporting roles (such as production assistant, producer's assistant, assistant coordinator and assistant director – many different terms for fetching coffee from Starbucks), while directing and producing independent music videos and short films, before absconding to travel and write. He has completed one novel, *Shoot The Runner*, and a collection of short stories. He is currently undertaking his second novel, while hoping to get the first one published at some point in the not-too-distant future. His short story 'The People's Republic' has recently been awarded both The Excellence in Contemporary Narrative Award and The Diamond Award in *The Labello Press* international short story competition and was published in *Gem Street: Collector's Edition*. Because of this, he is now unbearable to be around.

WELTSCHMERZ

Highly commended story, by Stephen Pollock

He was known as Mr Sudsy – the washing powder tsar of Yorkshire. People in the north-East were in awe of him, they regarded him as the Donald Trump of detergent. The nexus of his empire was Hull, Grimsby and Scunthorpe. Mr Sudsy called it his soapy Bermuda Triangle. It's rumoured that his personal fortune was in excess of £25-million.

Harold turned the page and continued to devour the

fat police dossier.

Mr Sudsy likes to dress up as Vera Lynn and eat bridies while prostitutes watch him masturbate. He claims to have slept with over 300 women. He is a sex addict, or as our generation like to call it, 'a mad shagger'. Phil Minker, Soap Suds regional manager.

The intercom on Harold's desk began to blink.

"Harold, Mrs Marigold is on the phone, she's asking if she can make an emergency appointment with you this morning?"

Harold sighed. "I had three sessions with her last week, what's wrong with her now?"

"She says the voices have come back and the begonia on her windowsill looks like Frank Bruno."

Harold groaned. "Book her in."

*

Harold assumed his favourite seat on the 5.15pm express train to Hull. He opened his leather attaché case – the same one he had carted around for 25 years – and placed the Sudsy case file on his lap. Where was he? Ah, yes, page five. Mr Sudsy had just abandoned his third wife and registered yet another business – Fishy Fries. Yorkshire's premier cod-flavoured snack. The fiasco was short-lived: Smiths, who owned Scampi Fries, initiated legal action and forced Fishy Fries into a bumbling retreat. Mr Sudsy retaliated by launching a range of Yorkshire-inspired sodas. The line included Red Bollocks and Miner's Yank, an energy drink containing burdock, mustard and Guarana.

Harold's chuckle attracted a glance from the seat opposite. He was normally tangled in *The Times* crossword by this point, somewhere between five across and an aneurysm, with a look of glazed resignation. The passenger tried to glimpse the case file, but Harold sensed the man's incursion and shifted his knee, shielding the file with his grey flannel-suit.

He scurried to the appendix, eager to find out what Mr Sudsy looked like. He was somewhat disappointed to find that Mr Sudsy was actually quite handsome, but not in the conventional sense: he had dense, curly brown hair, ruddy cheeks and a ten-bob smile. The clothes were Yorkshire Hollywood: chequered sports jacket, Paisley-pattern tie and a pair of tan bellbottoms. Harold's career had taught him that most lotharios were not overly attractive; they relied on psychological and vocal artillery. At the age of 14 Harold had discovered, to his eternal disappointment, that girls went for silverback gorillas, not pseudo-intellectuals. The man opposite peeked over his spread-eagled newspaper. Harold elevated his leg, bringing into view an old school photo of Mr Sudsy. He immediately recognised the sallow paint on the gymnasium wall. It couldn't be... sat on the front bench, with his hands clasped on top of his scuffed knees, was a timid Harold, wedged between the future mayor of Grimsby and a local dermatologist. Grinning on the back row was a young Mr Sudsy, surrounded by the class wags and his girlfriend Jenny (the only girl in primary seven to have nurtured two hummocks under her school jumper).

A violent jolt shoogled the train carriage and sprayed the contents of the case file onto the floor. The passenger opposite slipped off his seat and crouched on one knee.

"Allow me to help," said the nosy stranger.

"It's OK," blurted Harold, his grey face now flushed with emotion. "I can get them."

In the subsequent fumble, the school photo shot under the seat and disappeared beneath a carriage heater. The stranger continued to fuss.

"You know, we sit in the same carriage every day but we never talk. I'm Nigel. I work for Barnaby and Joyce Accountants in Grimsby."

"Harold, I work across the road at Sinker Psychiatry."

Harold reluctantly shook the man's hand, then scowled at the photo of Mr Sudsy trapped under his left Hush Puppy.

*

The bus that shuttled between Hull train station and Harold's middle-class tomb took around 40 minutes. He sat on the top deck, peering out at the muddy flats that flanked the River Ouse. He wondered if the boy in the school photograph was actually Mr Sudsy – the dolt who had teased him incessantly at school. Such parallels were easily drawn by a 48-year-old man, who, by virtue of age, would often find himself dissecting the past, rather than embracing the future. Harold drew a squeaky circle on the misted bus window. He peeked through the hole and saw his younger self playing tennis – strong, emerald eyes; palomino thighs and a pinch of steel...

*

Harold was brooding in his study with a large Glenlivet. His wife was next door, enjoying an episode of _Lewis_. The file peeped out of his attaché case, but Harold was determined to ignore it, and pretended to leaf through a periodical instead. Reading about Mr Sudsy's life reduced him to a dreary whimper. The phone on Harold's bureau began to jangle. It was his 'hot line' that clients rang in the event of an implosion; but recently Mrs Marigold had been pestering him with tales of a satanic gerbil.

"Mrs Marigold, how can I help?"

"Is that Harold Sinker?" said a male voice.

"Yes, whom am I speaking with?"

"I am an old friend of Mr Sudsy, I just wondered how you were getting on with his evaluation?"

Harold lent forward and rested his whisky on the desk's leather carapace.

"Sorry, I'm not at liberty to discuss that, patient-client confidentiality and the court case is pending, would you li–"

The calm voice interjected, "I'm sure you'll do a great job. In fact I think you'll find that Mr Sudsy has a mental condition that will absolve him of all responsibility."

Harold's single malt began to lap against the walls of his crystal glass.

"Do you think your shitty little practice got this case by accident?" continued the voice, this time with a slightly gruffer edge. "Mr Sudsy made sure that his evaluation came to you – his wimpy ex-classmate. You are going to help us out, Harold. You know it and so do I. You were always the last pick at football – things haven't changed."

"Wait a min–"

The phone line went dead. Harold sat in silence for several seconds before gulping down his nightcap. He reached across and plucked the case file from the attaché case.

Maybe the call was a hoax: one of his old classmates

who had seen the court listing in the *Grimsby Herald*. He galloped through the case file, until he reached a gory anecdote on page 52.

Although Mr Sudsy is predominantly a charmer and womaniser – he had kissed the Blarney Stone in his pampers – he has a predisposition for violence which can flare up at a moment's notice. During a Soap Suds sales conference in Cleethorpes, he bludgeoned an employee with a three-litre carton of detergent after catching him texting during a presentation. He went berserk and used any implement within reach as a cudgel – repeatedly whacking the man with a toilet brush, mop and sanitary towels. I will never forget that pink effervescence, as the blood mixed with soap powder on the boardroom floor. That day, he made Caligula look like Bill Oddie. Tony Furk, Soap Suds managing director.

A brief pillage of the case file revealed more violence and skirmishes. There were also dalliances with the Yorkshire underworld and a slew of unpaid alimonies. It seemed that the glare of the police had been on Mr Sudsy for some time, but his heavyweight political connections had always kept them at bay. Mr Sudsy wasn't just a rich farceur; he was a rich, violent farceur. There was always a hint of a fly undone, but now he was wielding a tyre iron in his right hand. Harold yanked open the bureau drawer and grasped his vial of valium.

*

Over the next fortnight Harold began to reread *Lolita*. During a torpid Sunday lunch with his wife (the kids had promised to come, but cancelled at the 11th hour again) he had begun to ponder Vladimir Nabokov's inspiration for the novel. He had been moved by a newspaper article – probably in some émigré broadsheet – that told of an ape that had been raised in captivity and taught to communicate and perform human tasks. When the ape was given a sheet of paper and a set of crayons, it sketched the bars on its cage. On hearing Nabokov describe the incident, Harold felt such empathy with the primate that he nearly burst into tears. However, his pity was tempered by his own reticence, and he only managed a dignified sniffle.

"Harold, would you like some more gravy?" enquired his wife from the stern of the dining table.

Harold gaped at the faded certificates and photos that peppered the walls. Now that his two daughters had left home, all that remained was the detritus of what had always been a flimsy marriage.

"Harold! Would you like some gravy?"

"No, I'm fine," he muttered, ushering some peas around his plate.

The ape lingered in Harold's brain; it wouldn't relent. He pictured himself drawing on a sheet of manila – he had sketched his iron bed frame, with a set of L-plates on the headboard.

"Good, Mr Ape Man," said the white-coated operative. "Now put the banana in the slot."

Harold wrested the keys from the zookeeper and bounded out the door.

"Harold, where are you going?" yelled his wife.

"The study! I need to phone Mr Sudsy."

*

The night before the trial arrived with the air of a doctor's waiting room, Harold was lying in bed with the case file strewn over his ill-fitting pyjamas. His right eyebrow twitched at will and two generous sweat patches adorned his oxters. He washed down a handful of diazepam with some tepid hot chocolate. The tension of the preceding weeks had induced vomiting, weight loss and chronic masturbation. He extended each of his fingers in sequence, trying in vain to tot up how many opiates he had taken that day. Finally, he regained some sangfroid, and peered down at the case file. A final skim would ensure there were no holes in his testimony. Despite the imminent risk of death or imprisonment, in some perverse way, he was actually starting to relish *The Adventures of Mr Sudsy*. It had all the reckless drama of the Old Testament. He thumbed to the lewd, page 72.

Sudsy would regularly hold orgies in his Alcázar in Scunthorpe. Everybody would attend: the local police commissioner, mayor, minor politicians, Russ Abbot—all of society's casualties. One party he waltzed in naked, wearing just cricket pads and brandishing a King Eddie cigar. He got everyone to slather themselves in baby oil and play Twister in the buff. No expense was spared and he hired Black Lace to play in the conservatory. I can distantly remember Mr Sudsy getting a reach around from a Maggie Philbin lookalike. Tom Tunt, Mr Sudsy's chauffeur.

Harold looked over at his pallid wife: the tight perm that vibrated with every passing snore, the washed-out nightie that hung off her shoulders like a Marks & Spencer's pall. In his twenties he had a wild fling with a Jamaican hussy at Hull University. He had wanted to marry her, but society and his parents disapproved. Instead he had settled for a Caucasian wallflower. He glared down at his wife's thin lips. He wondered if he should leave her behind tomorrow? Harold sighed, rolled onto his side, and quietly masturbated. He eventually reached a meek climax somewhere off the Caribbean coast.

*

The gentle shunt of the train lulled Harold into a state of childish bliss. Outside, the green countryside flashed by unannounced. Suddenly, his mobile phone began to vibrate. Harold tried to ignore it, but he wondered if it was the police — maybe they had caught up with him? He swiped the phone from the seat, squinted at the text message, and sighed. He started to tap a reply, but the words wouldn't flow. Since he had turned 45 the latency between his thoughts and fumbling prose had steadily grown. Eventually he ditched the fancy Latin and went for the jugular.

"Mrs Marigold, Harry Secombe died some time ago. In any case, he did not wear leather chaps and certainly did not waggle a purple dildo. Please take two valium and go straight to bed. I am going on a long holiday, please contact Dr Tartae in my absence."

The carriage door clattered open. Harold flinched. It was the train conductor: a tall man with a fat, inviting face. Harold fished the tickets out of his suit trousers and surrendered them with a nervous smile. The man inspected the tickets and quickly handed them back.

"Merci, Monsieur Sudsy."

Harold chuckled as the man retreated into the passageway. He sank into his seat and closed his eyes. He was glad his little ruse had worked: his false testimony had persuaded the jury to acquit Mr Sudsy on the grounds of mental illness — Harold fondled the leather briefcase on his lap. It was crammed with the money he had extorted from Mr Sudsy to lie in court. Later that day, his anonymous phone call to the police revealed that Mr Sudsy was an old classmate of his, making his testimony void and triggering a retrial. By this juncture he was already 500 miles south of Hull.

For the first time in years Harold felt a gentle throb in his undercarriage, a nubile flutter in his chest – the first pang of adolescence.

The carriage door clattered open again. Harold spun round. It was his wife, clutching an Eccles cake and a plastic cup of tea. She zigzagged across the carriage before lurching onto the seat beside him.

"I thought the Eurostar was meant to be smooth?" she protested.

She perched the cake on top of her Dick Francis novel, then slurped her milky tea.

"Does it rain much in Antibes? I forgot to pack my light jacket," she inquired, nibbling the perimeter of her cake.

"No, Vera, I don't think it rains much at all. I think the weather is going to be just fine."

~

Stephen Pollock's Biography

Stephen Pollock is originally from Glasgow in Scotland. In 2009 he moved to Australia, where he works as a journalist. He has had seven short stories published in various literary journals and publications, including *Regime* and *Cracked Eye*, and has won two UK short story competitions. He has also had poetry published in the *Brisbane Speed Poets Journal*. Most of his fiction is inspired by his former life in Glasgow, a city that throbs with drama and humour. He is currently putting the finishing touches to a novel set in Glasgow during the 1990s, amidst the backdrop of Cool Britannia. He enjoys Vladimir Nabokov's novels and the poetry of Sylvia Plath and Ted Hughes.

Contact Stephen at: stephenpolloc74@hotmail.com

SHORTLISTED STORIES

A MAN OF GREAT APPETITE

Shortlisted story, by Kerry Barner

Al walked into the room and smiled. The table was laden with food. Perfumed candles lined the mantelpiece, like soldiers fidgeting on watch. Manu Chao was playing at respectable levels on the bulbous CD player. Outside, it was raining heavily. The air was thick with lavender. He quickly assessed the situation. Salad stuff at one end, cheese, salami, olives and bread at the other. He positioned himself close to the Gorgonzola and took a slice of baguette in his hand. His wife, Mary, seated herself next to him.

"Dear, shouldn't you wait for the others first?" Her voice was soft and pleading.

Al put the baguette back in the basket and wiped his hands. He was hungry.

"Drink, Al?" asked the host.

"Please," said Al rather more quickly than he'd intended.

"Wine?"

"Please. A glass of red, please," said Al, anticipating his host's next move. Mary put her hand over his arm and squeezed it. Her fingers left marks in Al's flesh.

More people entered the room. Mary stood up to greet them. Al took the opportunity to grab a handful of nuts and shove them in his mouth. One of the new arrivals, a woman, made her way towards Al. She looked familiar. Nut dust had stuck to his sweaty palm. The woman took her hand in his and said, "Gloria."

"Al," he mumbled. A bit of nut shot through the gap in his teeth and lodged on her left breast. It glared back at him. Instinctively he reached out to wipe it away.

"What do you think you're doing?"

"Sorry, I was just... you had a bit of... you know, a crumb on your... dress."

Mary came up to them both, and linked arms with Al. "Have you met?"

Gloria gave him an I-know-your-game look. "Last year's Christmas party. Al was singing karaoke, if I remember rightly. The Smiths. 'Heaven Knows I'm Miserable Now'. A real crowd pleaser." She turned on her heel and marched off to join the others.

Mary giggled. "You do love that song, don't you, Al? Gloria's in HR," she whispered. "Going through a divorce right now. It's all got a bit toxic."

Al sat down. He was feeling weak at the knees. He hadn't eaten since lunch, almost three hours ago. The host handed over a glass of red filled almost to the brim and he took a large gulp. Bless her heart, he thought. The house cat, a fluffy Persian named Lucinda, rubbed against the table leg and looked up at him. Al pursed his lips at it and made a kissing sound. The cat leapt into his lap and started to claw at his trousers. It was preparing to make itself comfortable. Al let one go gently. The cat stopped in its tracks and darted from him, her tail upright. Lucinda turned at the doorway and fixed her green eyes on him. I know your game, she seemed to say.

"That's funny," said Mary. "Cats usually love you." The sour smell caught her nostrils. "Oh, Al," she said. "Really."

"It was the cat," Al said weakly.

"My eye." Mary walked off to talk to the other guests, her movements remarkably like the cat's.

All backs were turned. Al grabbed the knife, carved a huge triangle of Gorgonzola, slapped it on the sliced baguette and lobbed the whole thing in his mouth in one go. His cheeks bulged as he tried to manoeuvre the cheese to a better position. Some was stuck on his palate. He swirled his tongue round the side but it lodged at the back of his throat. He started to choke. Mary ran to his side. "Are you OK, dear?" Al pointed to his mouth and gestured with his hands for water. She handed him a glass.

"Is everything all right?" asked the host.

"Food," said Al, coming up for air. "Went down the wrong way."

"For a second I thought it was my cooking."

"Not at all," said Mary. "The food looks delicious. Al

can vouch for that. He's tried most plates already, haven't you, dear?"

"Excellent," said the host. "I like to see a man enjoying his food. Tuck in, Al. Come on everyone. Help yourself."

The rest of the guests gathered round the table. Gloria sat close to the lettuce bowl. A lesbian couple, one with red hair, one with peroxide blonde, fed olives and grapes to each other. It made Al think of the fairy tale, 'Snow White and Rose Red'. The host handed round more drinks while deftly polishing off three glasses herself. Al was on his second block of cheese when he looked up at the stairway. Lucinda had poked her head through the spindles, her green eyes fixed on him. All of a sudden he felt guilty. He clenched his buttocks together. He needed the toilet but would Lucinda let him pass? Lucinda stretched her front paw like a ballerina, licking it delicately. She worked on the next paw, then yawned widely. Her teeth looked sharp.

Al stood up.

"What's the matter, dear?" asked Mary. "You look like you've seen a ghost."

"Think I'll go for a cigarette," he said.

It was still raining outside. Al lit up and inhaled deeply. The garden was very orderly. A wooden path led to a large shed. Along the base of the path were lavender plants, interspersed with basil, sage, rosemary and chives. A bumblebee hovered over one of the lavender flowers. A fat raindrop landed on its back and it buzzed away angrily. Al looked up at the first floor. He could see the frosted window of the bathroom. A nose was pressed against it. Was that Lucinda watching him? He looked through the patio doors but couldn't see any guests. What if he relieved himself here in the garden?

No one would notice. He sauntered nonchalantly to the shed and patted the wooden door as though marking his approval. Leaning his head round the side he could just about squeeze into the gap. He undid his belt and was about to pull down his trousers when he heard, "What do you think you're doing?"

It was Gloria.

He buckled up quickly, and turned to her.

"Nothing. Just... checking the frame for mould." He patted the side of the shed as though vouching for this solid piece of workmanship. "Do you have a shed?" It was a dumb question. Gloria ignored it.

"Do you have a spare cigarette?" she asked.

"Yes, yes, of course. Here, take two."

"Just the one, thanks," said Gloria. Her long red nails reached for the packet.

"My husband, my soon-to-be ex-husband, is the gardener. I prefer indoor pursuits."

Al imagined her naked, whip in hand, scoring his bare back until she drew blood. He took another cigarette from the pack. His hand shook.

"You seem nervous?" asked Gloria.

"It's the rain. It makes me shiver."

"I've been watching you, you know. You're a man of great appetite."

Al looked back at the house. Lucinda had moved again. She was now blocking the doorway. Her head seemed to have doubled in size, and she was looking straight at him. Did she just wink?

"Do you like cats?" he said rather desperately.

"There's only one animal that interests me," said Gloria, taking a long drag and blowing the smoke up in the air. Al felt sure she meant men.

"I've never been much of a cat person," said Al.

"Mary tells me that cats love me. But I don't love them back. Do you think that's wrong of me? Take this cat. I feel that it's been watching me ever since I arrived."

"Maybe it's your smell."

"I beg your pardon."

"Cats are attracted and repulsed by a human's scent."

Al felt guilty again. For a second he couldn't see Lucinda anywhere. The coast was clear. He would make it into the house, up to the bathroom and finish what he started at the back of the shed.

"Excuse me," he said and stubbed his cigarette on the floor. It left a black mark on the wooden path. He started to run. At the doorstep, he took a giant leap, hoping to scale the threshold. Lucinda crossed the kitchen floor just as Al's boot made contact with the granite tiling. There was a yelp. He'd trodden on Lucinda's tail. They both skidded across the room, Lucinda clawing and scratching in self-defence.

"What do you think you're doing?" It was Gloria again, framed in the doorway. Al could taste blood. He'd bitten his tongue on landing and now his left cheek was smarting.

"I... missed the step. Fell on the cat."

Mary appeared from the living room. "Al, what happened?"

"It was an accident," he said. "I think she might be hurt."

"Who?"

"It's not the cat you need to worry about," said Gloria, stepping over Al's sprawled body. Al looked up. She was not wearing any panties. Al felt a lurch in his groin. He rolled to one side to hide the growing bulge. Mary squatted down beside him and said, "Al?" He shrugged and mouthed the word 'divorce' silently.

The host appeared with a napkin in one hand and a half-full glass of red in the other. The wine sloshed about wildly as she bent down towards Al. Some of it spilt onto Al's trousers. He pretended not to notice.

"Here, take this for your face," said the host, handing Al the napkin. "Lucinda'll survive. She's tougher than you think, you know. Between you and me, I think she has a bit of a vindictive streak. If I'm tottering up to bed after a jar too many, she always seems to be at the top of the stairs. Watching. There's something judgemental about that poise of hers. And just as I get to the step where she's sitting, she sticks her leg out to lick it. As though she's trying to trip me up. I swear, I've nearly come a-cropper over the years. Here, let me help you up."

The host tugged at his sleeve and spilled more wine over Al's arm. Al's erection was beginning to hurt.

"Think I'll just freshen up. That's where I was heading when I... when Lucinda... when we collided."

"Of course, of course!" shouted the host, dusting down Al's trouser leg. She caught sight of his crotch and smiled knowingly. "Top of the stairs, first left. The light switch is on the outside. Take your time."

Al daubed his trousers. The napkin soaked up the wine like a bloodstain. He put his hand on the banister and looked up. There she was: Lucinda. At the top of the stairs looking down on him. He'd have to walk past her. Her tail flicked in accusation. How should he approach her? Cautiously? At a run? He decided to go gently, one step at a time, hoping to gauge which way she might turn. He was one step below her. The green eyes had followed his every move. He made a kissing sound to appease her. Lucinda did not react. Slowly –

oh, so slowly – he lifted his leg over the cat's head. Not a movement. He raised the second leg up and over. Still no reaction. He'd made it safely over the feline hurdle. He felt like an Olympic champion.

His urge to relieve himself was so strong that he burst into the bathroom without turning on the light. There was no time to turn the lock, no time to lift the toilet seat. He unzipped his flies and aimed into the bathtub.

The light went on.

The door handle turned.

Gloria entered, followed by Lucinda. Gloria gazed at Al. Her eyes were green. She stuck out her leg and tripped Al up. As he lay on the floor, Lucinda leapt onto his chest, put her nose against his and said, "What do you think you're doing?"

~

Kerry Barner's Biography

Kerry Barner was born in Yorkshire in the north of England, but has lived in London for 20 years. She is a commissioning editor for an international academic publisher. In 2009 she was shortlisted for *Wasafiri's* New Writer Prize and her work has appeared in *Brand literary magazine*, *Notes From The Underground*, *Anthropology and Humanism*, *Spilling Ink Review*, *The Bicycle Review* and the *Momaya Annual Review 2012*. In 2011 she co-founded *The Short Story* competition and now runs it solo. In June 2014 she published the first anthology of *Best of The Short Story*. Loves dogs, hates mashed potato.

Kerry's website: www.theshortstory.net

BUILDERS FROM HUELL

Shortlisted story, by Polly Ann White

She saw herself as a person of quiet disposition, with abundant patience, always calm when confronted by calamity. Indeed, her temper was never stretched to snapping, nor did she ever succumb to chucking artefacts through the window or swearing uncontrollably. Her favourite pastime was playing a hushed game of Scrabble.

June

The day was already suffused with vitality – buds bursting, lambs bleating, birds tweeting (in the avian manner). The sky was a cloudless blue, the sun a blinding yellow. Little daisies on the village green were releasing their tightly closed petals and nodding cheerfully. Later they would be crushed by heavy building equipment but during this delightful moment of promise, all was ignorant bliss.

The previous evening she had drunk a small glass of Prosecco in celebration of the forthcoming day because very shortly, after two years of physical discomfort and regular visits from the angel of gloom, she could rid herself of candles, black bin-liners taped across broken windows and the scorched pan standing on the fire trivet, black as black and in desperate need of a controllable hob, or the tip.

Transformation was imminent. And here they were, the little band of builders from the fair city Huell (with its tree-lined avenues) anxious to start, ready to turn her ancient house into to a modern home. With joyful expectation she unbolted, unchained and unlocked the 300-year-old door.

Alas, the three persons who stood before her, whose faces resembled a fearsome trio of gargoyles, were... an ineffable disappointment. Her heart sank, but only slightly, not to the very bottom because, initial judgements often require further analysis and a peculiar countenance does not always signify insanity. She smiled weakly and said how nice it was to see them all. They introduced themselves.

"I'm Dave, luv," said the first with an air of assertiveness.

"Dave," mumbled the next.

"Dave," said the third, examining his mismatched, bashed-up boots.

She realised immediately that identical names would cause confusion so, after a short discussion, principally her own because their vocabulary was limited, she appropriated D-one, D-two and D-three.

The latter was a fat chap whose midriff spilled over in two dough-like undulations. He was the skivvy and owned a pronounced speech impediment which was accompanied by a fine spray of saliva. She was never near enough to see the colour of his eyes but they were sunk deeply into his bulging face and suspiciously close together.

During the first five minutes of awkward preamble, the two-syllabled names were reduced to the rudimentary form of ONE, TWO and THREE or collectively, the D's.

ONE was of average height and build. He proclaimed his superiority but the lamentable gap at the front of his floppy mouth somehow diminished his self-appointed station, as did the attempted comb-over. From the fowl bursts of oral odour she gathered he was a frequent imbiber of the beer. His front teeth may have been removed by advanced decay or the force of a fist, but this minor disfigurement also led to (unfortunate coincidence) a discharge of saliva, though more of a dribble than a spray. And, he had two digits missing from his left hand. (Careless, possibly?)

"Where is the foreman?" she asked politely.

"Ee's brok' 'is toes. Yeh, three of 'em."

"Oh, I'm so sorry. How did it happen?"

"Dropped a barrel of ale on 'em."

"Ooh painful. He wasn't at work then?"

"Yeh, we was demolishin' t'old brewery. We only nicked a couple."

"When will he be coming do you suppose?"

"Not sure, luv, not sure. Brok' toes are bad as a brok' leg."

"Yes," she said, finding it difficult to hide a twinge of apprehension, "I understand, small fractures can be just as debilitating."

The sky maintained its blue hue and the sun continued its bright trajectory. But the minute she had retreated into the hall, hovering nervously on the ninth stair, the D's dragged in their builders' paraphernalia and proceeded to pummel away at the hall walls. Using the most aggressive apparatus they extracted great lumps of plaster which fell to the floor like dead dogs. She stood in trepidation, fearing that the ceiling would collapse and compromise the surface of her rare terracotta floor tiles. She wondered if the D's really knew what they were doing. Would the Listed Buildings Officer permit such a crude and random offence to her house, which incidentally, she had grown to love, despite its frowsty smells and lack of basic amenities. These were the first walls they had seen. There had been no preparation for this casual onslaught, not one protective sheet. She had anticipated at the very least a consulted 'To Do' list. Her piano was being unceremoniously shoved from one side of the room to the other; her crockery, still stored in cardboard boxes, was spinning across the floor; suitcases bursting with clothes (due to the lack of a wardrobe) were spilling their contents and would probably be used as builders' rags. She sat down, put her head in her hands, a finger in each ear, felt her heart sink again, almost to the bottom and was gradually covered by a layer of fine, white dust which contained substantial bits of chipped brick.

"TWO," yelled ONE, looking up at her and thumbing towards his workmate, "is a awesome plasterer an' a awesome plumber."

Meaningless words at present, she thought. TWO had as many ear piercings as would fit in such small lobes. He also displayed an eyebrow bar, a nose ring and a black cheek stud which had the look of an escaped bogey. These facial decorations seemed incongruous. Though extremely agile, bobbing and twisting, he was not at all flamboyant but reticent, too quiet. In fact he rarely spoke, apart from the occasional muttered answer to a query, which she was eventually able to interpret by the number of rapid movements on the lid of his left eye (truly). A few twitches denoted a positive response and a plethora indicated a negative. This basic method of communication often simplified matters but she did feel that her future with this trio of dubious D's was looking questionable.

August

In the fullness of time she learned that the D's hailed from one of the less salubrious areas of the city, the Blandshome Estate. Apparently an area reputed to be rife with scoundrels and serial killers, a frightening place, to be avoided... and she now had three of its tenants under her roof.

"Ar lass is 'avin' a bairn," said ONE discursively as she proffered a mug of builder's tea.

"Oh how lovely. Congratulations. How many children do you have?"

"Six," he said with some pride.

"Gosh! Quite a handful. Are they all at school?"

"Yeh. Ar Brandy's 'avin' a bairn too."

"Oh! Very nice. And who is Brandy?"

"Ma eldest kid, she's fotteen but 'er lad's a good'n, ee'll do 'er right. Ee's not kid's fatha, but ee'll do 'er right."

"Well… that's very commendable. How old is her boyfriend?"

"Which'n?"

"The one who's going to stand by her."

"Fifteen. Just 'ad a new set a teef. Good'ns, real good'ns, white as a rabbit's ass, drinks like a fuckin' fish. Great lad."

She walked away, deep in distressing thought – illegal intercourse… mother and daughter under the same roof with toothless, dribbling husbands and babies… and how very disagreeable to procreate with…

Being quite oblivious to her surroundings at that moment, she fell on top of THREE who was removing a piece of wainscot.

"Fuckin' 'ell. Fuckin' bloody 'ell."

He remained static so she straddled awkwardly over his fat back, whose width and doughy consistency prevented serious injury to both. He repeated the exclamation several times, quite needlessly she thought.

"I'm so sorry," she said peering down at him. "Are you alright?"

"Dun fuckin' back in, ya clumsy cow."

She was a little surprised at his vociferous reaction. "Oh dear, shall I bring the others to haul you up?"

TWO dropped his sledge hammer and came dashing over to the injured man. He seemed very adept at straightening bent bodies, probably, she thought, due to his agility and innate strength and also his twitching eye, which might initiate any number of unfortunate incidents when associating with his pals at the pub. It took less than five minutes, with much cracking of bones, discernible even under excessive flesh, and THREE was upright then ready to be driven home, to convalesce, with as many cans of ale as would anaesthetise his back, for an unspecified duration.

October

Renovation progressed and regressed in equal measure. At this stage the walls were denuded of old plaster. Window frames and rotten floorboards had been removed. (The latter were laid on a compressed mixture of soil, cinders and small skeletons.) New pipes and wires were beginning to be assembled.

When THREE did return, looking plumper, sounding less coherent and with a childlike vagueness, he brought with him a spade and pickaxe. Several days later, on returning from work, she noticed a deep, un-shapely hole in the garden.

"Thought ya should 'av' a pond," he said smiling with self-regard.

She studied the gaping crater.

"Thank you," she said, noticing a little displeasure creeping into her tone, "but I didn't ask for a pond. I had other plans for the garden and anyway, where was the notification, the prior discussion?" He looked puzzled.

She closed her eyes and sighed deeply.

During the next few weeks the pit was filled with builders' detritus which eventually grew into a sizeable hillock.

The building inspector came at regular intervals to

check progress. During one of his visits he commended the builders on their workmanship regarding the installation of the bathroom Yorkshire Lights (small sliding windows, replicas of the originals) but pointed out that the glass should be frosted, obscured, (processed into an appealing texture of seething maggots) despite the fact that the next house was 25 meters away and the gardens were divided by a row of rampaging Leylandii. Not wanting to relinquish the potential view of a productive vegetable plot, she felt that the inspector might be deceived by applying self-adhesive vinyl window film, (complete with busy floral design) over the plain glass which could be ripped off when he had paid his last visit. This she did with patient precision, carefully inserting a scalpel along the edges of the frame to ensure a perfect fit. The builders were impressed. Fortunate then, that the film was securely in place when THREE inadvertently put a ladder through the window while removing flaking bricks from the outside wall. His explanation was too garbled to be understood, even the string of violent curses dissolved into meaningless jabber, but the shattered glass remained intact, stuck with admirable tenacity to the film, hanging onto the frame by one corner as if a modern design for stained glass had just blown in.

Had there been a pond in the garden after this event, she might have been tempted to push THREE into it, gently, with just the tip of her little finger.

December

Now that all the old beams had been exposed, thoroughly perforated by the ticking Death Watch beetle, a new person was employed. ONE introduced him while simultaneously miming the use of a machine gun.

"Ee's 'ere to spray livin' daylights out a fuckin' bastards," he cheerfully explained.

The new man had an amiable face, a winsome smile and a bob of fair hair. What a pleasant change she thought. He entered the house with his spraying equipment and seeing that she was struggling with a bag of rubble, offered to assist. He continued to help with three more bags (she was often left to clear the rubbish). Such kindness, she thought, suggesting he might fancy a nice mug of tea and choccy biscuits. After replenishment she led him up to the attic where he was to start spraying.

"Right lass, you start 'ere, I'll clear out bedrooms."

She stared at him as he began to divide the tools. "Pardon!"

"Yep, one good'n deserves another. I 'elped ya wit' trash."

"What!"

"Yep, let's get fuckin' crackin'."

She was incapable of speech, baffled, bewildered.

It is true that she was becoming accustomed to the reversal of minor roles (the builders occasionally made their own tea) and to hearing a succession of profanities, daily, if not hourly but really, the audacity... and without warning she was suddenly overwhelmed by a whooshing sensation, a great releasing of stifled frustration and, grabbing the nearest object, she flung it across the room with monumental gusto. Fortunately the appalling man (looks are actually *very* deceptive) ducked before the iron bedpost (not valuable) smashed into his head. Suppressed tears were liberated as she slammed the attic door and ran down the stairs. On reaching the bottom, a little calmer, she had a niggling fear that the newcomer might perform the builder's equivalent of 'spitting in the soup'.

*

It was mid-December. She was no cynic, the exuberance of the festive season never failed to excite her, even during this time of cataclysmic disruption. She had just returned home after late-night shopping, which included small appropriate gifts for each of the three D's. As the door was pushed open she noticed a mass of rubble in the hall corner, no doubt waiting for her to 'bag up'. Looking more closely, in the dim light of an old 25w bulb, she deciphered the shapes of a pair of upturned wellingtons and farther along, two grimy rubber gloves, all protruding timidly from the pile.

"Oh my god!" she whispered, "Oh my god."

Thoughts whirring, how dreadful... how distressing... to die in such a manner... crushed by the dregs of his trade... his poor family... and just before Christmas... an ambulance, quickly... police... health & safety officers... the building inspector... an enquiry... the house would never be finished. She hesitated for a moment and then moved closer to the victim. Thinking it would be preferable to discover a stiff finger rather than a whole stiff foot, she tentatively prodded the gritty rubber then, having gained a little more confidence, squeezed with increasing pressure. Oh relief! Blessed relief. The finger was empty.

She stood up slowly, pondering. This was a joke, the builders' Christmas joke, a cruel and tasteless jest. But after moments of anger, she began to smile.

February

Electricity was still a great novelty and she clicked the dangling light switches with giddy abandon. In the drawing room (for some reason still without power) the floor was being excavated and a series of planks had been arranged to allow access to other rooms. One evening she attempted to traverse the makeshift support carrying a bag of groceries and a lighted candle. The candle fell (inevitably) still lit, and rolled under the planks. An immediate, immense conflagration was envisioned so she descended into the cavity, spilling (inevitably) the contents of the carrier. After much tenuous groping she managed to retrieve all the items, including the candle, and struggled towards terra firma, begrimed, dishevelled and very cold.

In order to obtain hot water the old range fire needed to burn for at least five hours, so bathing at 9pm was an impossibility, but there was a battered electric kettle in the scullery. She boiled water to wash, looking forward to her nightly G&T (used as a medicinal restorative, the bottle and glass were secreted under her bed. This habit had started a month after the builders' arrival.)

Her yearning at this juncture was to have a real bathroom with buttermilk walls – the delicate colour of winter sun, and an open shelf piled with neatly folded, pale blue, soft and fluffy, Egyptian cotton towels. It was such an ardent longing, pervading many of her agitated dreams.

When she entered her bedroom after the cursory wash, she saw with incredulity that the D's had not only dismantled the ceiling but also removed the small roof, in its entirety. (It was 5° below.) She scrambled frantically for the restorative thinking that alcohol might increase her rapidly diminishing temperature. After downing three glasses, still fully clothed, she pulled on her uber-thick dressing gown and snuggled down for the night. Trying desperately to focus on an area just above her head, she realised that the builders had at least had the foresight to stretch several strips of cling film across the beams directly above her pillow, presumably to prevent fatal pneumonia should freezing rain or snow prevail.

Depressed sighs were becoming ever more frequent. But the sky was clear and her life-saving electric blanket was emitting a comforting warmth. As she peeped over the blankets at the slightly blurred sliver of silver moon and twinkling stars, she thought, *what a wonderful adventure... life is really terribly... good and very...* Then she sank (aided by the restorative) into a blissful state of sleep.

*

Perhaps to compensate for his restrained verbal interchange TWO occasionally demonstrated panache and dexterity. He was elfin-like, a lightweight, small and sinewy. With his plasterer's hawk, skimming trowel, feather edge and internal corner trowel he would deftly prance in front of a newly surfaced wall and produce a three dimensional floral arrangement, not dissimilar to high calibre stuccowork. Such artistry was a wonder to behold. Her only concern was that after he had received well deserved praise, he might scuttle off to an urgent plumbing problem and she would be left with the lovely but inappropriate art work. Fortunately this only happened once when a blossoming Easter wreath had to be chipped away and the whole wall re-plastered. On other occasions he always managed to eradicate the design with swift swipes of his finishing trowel before it went off.

As an acknowledged drunkard ONE often arrived late morning in a state of extended intoxication. On a particularly dismal day, when TWO had just skimmed his final wall, ONE sloped into the room, bleary eyed, with a slight tremor, looking extremely pale and possibly close to death. She was concerned (another possible corpse on the premises would have been unendurable) and proposed a strong mug of tea and a hearty breakfast. At this suggestion he projectile vomited, fell back against the pristine wall and slid to the floor, taking a length of soft plaster with him.

To her consternation he remained in a state of unconsciousness for the next few hours. THREE covered the soporific body with a used cement bag and insisted on placing a mirror under the nose at regular intervals while she attempted to remove the splattered contents of the stomach.

Eventually, the entity stirred and released resounding notes of wind, almost certainly flammable.

"How do you feel?" she said, gagging but with some empathy.

"Fuckin' fucked."

He slumped deeper into the wall and returned to clueless oblivion.

She scrutinised the large realistic arachnids tattooed on each side of his neck. They made her wonder if, in the darkness of night, the two spiders came to life (the mind often drifts under extreme stress) and crawled through the hole left by his four absent incisors. She had noted that after evenings of excessive drinking he produced loud snorting noises caused by vibrations of the soft palate. Remembrance of this put a stop to her silly imaginings – the spiders would have been expelled at some speed to become inclusions in the newly plastered walls.

After an interminable period having to endure foul smelling emissions, she suggested to THREE that he might gently rouse ONE and take him home. He acquiesced with enthusiasm (his back obviously now in good order) and dragging the flaccid ONE to the front door, along with a trail of crushed plaster, said that they would be back, 'bright 'n breezy' the following morning.

In fact they did not return until the following fortnight and when she questioned the length of their absenteeism, "Stuck in fuckin' traffic," was their unified rejoinder.

April

The warmth of the sun gave brief solace. New windows had been fitted, new floors laid, a bathroom installed. She now had electricity throughout and with gas piped to the house, could experience the double bliss of central heating *and* magical open fires. But she was weary, so weary.

The D's were roofing and trying to reinstate the scullery chimney which had wobbled while they were applying strips of lead. She heard the crash and the frenzied squawks of chickens. Bricks and mortar had fallen into the neighbour's garden and killed three of his hens. He was, conveniently, taking an early holiday and anyway, they weren't on friendly terms because TWO had kicked his cat while it was releasing its business in her garden. The neighbour witnessed the assault from his ladders (he was cleaning his windows) and threatened TWO with a whopping stiff-bristled yard brush. (The cat now has the use of only three legs and is incapable of climbing the wall to perform its doings amidst the Dahlias, thank goodness.) Immediately after the regrettable chimney episode ONE suggested he retrieve the feathered cadavers and she should pluck, gut and cook them for the following day's butties. He also proposed *borrowing* some of the eggs.

Nearly June

The D's were now almost finished and it was enough. The last event, the regrettable demise of the luckless chickens, was the final straw. She was close to breakdown, could take no more. Crushed by the constant clamour of metallic tools, drills, hammers, Radio 2, the grit and the filth; drained of fortitude by perpetual anxiety; weakened by the prolonged effort of trying to be nice while having to listen to the ubiquitous expletive. The end must come soon.

June

And it did. A year, a whole year to the day and those gargoyles were packing up their gear and saying their goodbyes. She was numb, felt nothing. As she waved them off, THREE, not known for his tact, turned and said, "See ya when it all goes belly up."

They all laughed heartily.

ONE said, "An' don't ya be 'avin' them notes published. We've seen ya scribbling an' takin' snaps."

"Yeh," said THREE, twitching frantically, having at last become vocal, "an' we know where ya lives."

They all laughed again, with even more unfettered heartiness.

She smiled and whispered, "You dreadfully useless fucking freaks. Fuck off. I never want to see your fucked-up faces again. EVER."

Breathing heavily she closed the door and swore that she would never swear again, (although it had been rather pleasant).

After several minutes of insensibility, out of the blue, the clear blue sky, she felt a joyful uplifting – she was alone, there was silence, it was realised, this was *her* house and would become *her* home. With unbounded energy she sprinted to the pantry and retrieved a hidden bottle of Bollinger sent from her beloved brothers for this very occasion.

Once more she sat on the ninth stair, just as she had a year ago and, in the spirit of celebration, became blissfully blotto.

The Present

She now has a beautiful home, a thriving garden and a lively half-moon pond full of plopping frogs and wee aquatic beasties. Her singing (just a short burst to welcome each day) can be heard by the neighbour, who has never complained.

She often thinks fondly of the D's and their little joke with the wellies in the rubble.

And whenever she leaves home, she presses her palm against the hall wall, as a gesture of love, a way of saying, "I hope I will return safely, to this lovely place, which I will always cherish and never leave, except in a coffin, carefully constructed from the old scullery floorboards."

This moving maxim is uttered each time she steps over the threshold, even when it's only to nip round to the neighbour for their weekly supper, wine and Scrabble.

~

Polly Ann White's Biography

Born in Hampshire I now live in Yorkshire and have four children, 12 grandchildren and countless chickens.

I taught Graphic Design and Mixed Media for 20 years and have over 40 nonfiction books published, plus one illustrated children's book, translated into Japanese.

I used to write for the Yorkshire Post Women's Page but ceased after 18 months because the fees were abysmal, it being Yorkshire.

Last year I was short listed for the *London Magazine* annual short story competition.

Attempting to write fiction is a compulsive disorder, tempered only by trying to maintain a modicum of self-belief in the face of crushing rejection. My confidence breathes in one area of literature but has croaked in the other.

My time is spent (after essential eating and 'over the yardarm' libation) writing, painting, printmaking, gardening, organising the rota for Weekend Grandchildren and occasionally whipping round the house with a feather duster. I listen to the *Archers*, always anticipating the annihilation of Ambridge via a colossal sinkhole. Hence, unending disappointment.

I am hoping to live, faculties intact, to the age of 108, still writing, painting and generally having an uproarious

time.
I am profoundly grateful for my life thus far.

NEW YEAR REVOLUTION

Shortlisted story, by Sue Powis

8.30am

Margaret gazed at the sad plastic tree, the dusty paper chains and the battery-operated gyrating Santa which regaled everyone with, "Ho-ho-ho! And a Merrryyyyy Carrrrrismas!" whilst doling out static shocks courtesy of his fibre-optic beard. Mr Upjohn bought one decoration each year for the staffroom and the electrifying Santa was this year's contribution.

That some people decorated their houses many weeks before Christmas served to enhance the Festive Season by creating an atmosphere of anticipation; but, after Boxing Day, all decorations – especially those involving Santa – seemed so utterly pointless.

Margaret Phillips, Mr Upjohn's fiercely efficient personal assistant (known as Miss Marple behind her back but Mrs P to her face) wasn't one for Christmas at the best of times. Not that she was a bah-humbug kind of person, because she wasn't. It was just that Christmas for her was neither the season to be jolly nor did it resemble a holiday in even the loosest of terms. Christmas Day meant an endless cycle of food preparation, washing-up and listening to the disjointed stories trotted out by her hard-of-hearing father whose grasp on reality was tenuous at best. Boxing Day meant more food with the added bonus of endless hours of football at 120 decibels.

These days Margaret didn't even have the pleasure of the company of the grandchildren, whose presence had always made Christmas so enjoyable. For the past five years, her son and daughter-in-law – both keen snowboarders – had whisked their offspring away on holiday to the Alps the day after the schools broke up and returned the day before the new term began. Despite their heartfelt apologies, she told them that she didn't blame them in the slightest and told them to go and enjoy themselves. They had very many wonderful times together over the year. But not having them around made Christmas Dinner 'with all the trimmings' with Dad and Bob feel like an overblown Sunday lunch with a holly-and-candle table decoration and a stodgy pudding with brandy butter (which she hated but pushed a tablespoon around the bowl and pretended to eat because it was easier than having to explain to her father, yet again, why she was eating a tangerine).

*

Unable to abide the jaded decorations a moment longer, Margaret began to dismantle the tree.

"Mrs P! What *are* you doing?" Cally practically screamed. "It's bad luck to take down Christmas decorations before the sixth!"

"You are mistaken. It's bad luck to have them up *after* the sixth," Margaret replied calmly as she continued to denude the tree of its ugly, shatterproof decorations.

"Mrs P! Please!" Cally implored as she attempted to wrest the box of gaudy baubles from Margaret's hand.

"Either I take them down now or you'll be doing it on your own tomorrow evening. But tomorrow is the night you have your tap-dance-yourself-to-mental-agility class after work, isn't it? So how you'll manage to be in two places at once, I really don't know. But manage you will have to because..." Margaret paused and smiled sweetly, "it will be *your* fault, California Jackson, if the spirit of bad luck that you seem to think hatches out of inert Christmas decorations on the seventh of January haunts us for the entire year."

"Whatever!" Cally huffed as she strode off to the packing department.

Moments after Cally's departure, Margaret found it impossible not to laugh out loud when, after a few alarming burbling noises, the shocking Santa's head fell off to reveal a metal spike of such dangerous proportions that she, as Health and Safety Officer, felt duty-bound to report to Mr Upjohn. As she strode off in search of the supplier of potentially lethal Christmas novelties, Margaret was grinning from ear to ear.

12.30pm

"What did Josh buy you for Christmas, Cal?" Becci asked.

"A gold bracelet and a coat, but I chose them myself. I can't trust him to buy anything as he's not very good at such things. What did Steve get for you?"

(Actually what they said was: "Wotcha gerroff Josh, Cal?" "A gold bracele' an' a coa', but I chose bofe. I carnt trust 'im to buy nuffink as 'e's bleedin' useless. Wotcha gerroff Steve?")

Margaret had learned to ignore their irritating vowel syndrome, their inability to pronounce 'th' and the woeful dearth of the letter 't'. The circuit in her head that translated Cally/Becci speech into a facsimile of English was in such fine working order that she had even stopped grinding her teeth, which was good news regarding her dental bill.

"I got these…" Becci replied, pulling back her long, tiger-striped hair to reveal two pairs of enormous golden hoops. "And after all that food round me Mum's I got this belly, an' all!" she moaned, stretching the welt of her sweater over the soft roundness which constituted a normal female body. "I look as if I'm six months gone."

When I was six months pregnant you needed a map and compass to circumnavigate my bulge, Margaret mused as she munched on a celery stick.

"Bloody hell!" Cally exclaimed, biting into a rice cake and looking as if she was actually enjoying it. "How much weight you put on over the holidays?"

103

"Half a kilo."

Half a kilo! Just over a pound!! A measly pound and a bit!!!

"What about you, Cal? You put on any weight?"

"I lost three."

"Yore 'avin' me on! You lost three Ks? How?"

Yes, how?

"I got food poisoning on Christmas Eve from a dodgy doner off of that skuzzy kebab van by the park. I spent all Christmas Day in the lav. I only started eating properly on New Year's Eve and then me and Josh went clubbing. I got hammered and spent New Year's Day throwing up. I've only eaten rice cakes and drunk water most of the holiday."

"You lucky thing!" Becci commented seriously before turning to Margaret who was now nibbling on a carrot baton. "So, Mrs P... What did *you* get for Christmas?"

"Oh, this and that," Margaret replied vaguely.

This and that included a diary insert for her Filofax – something she got every year, which was fine because it saved her having to buy it herself; oven gloves – something she got every year because Bob invariably ruined several pairs throughout a normal year in the course of some DIY project; a lavender bath set – something she got every year despite loathing lavender as it reminded her of her acid-tongued and thoroughly dislikeable great-aunt who had spent her final years wearing a permanent sneer, far too much badly-applied make-up, a bright ginger wig and enough lavender toilet water to make your eyes smart; a pasting table, as one of the legs had fallen off the old one and decorating was in the offing; and a toilet seat. Yes, her husband of 37 years had presented her with a gift-wrapped toilet seat.

"What kind of this and that?" Cally pressed.

"A spa weekend with all the treatments," Margaret blurted.

Good God! Where had that come from?

"Oooh! You lucky thing! When are you going?"

"I'm not quite sure. It's a secret."

Damn right it was.

5.45pm

"Maggie. Glad you're home, love. Bit of a bad day, I'm afraid. The cat was sick on the living room rug."

"And you cleaned it up?"

Bob's head appeared over the banister. "Sorry. I've been far too busy fitting your toilet seat."

Great. Absolutely great...

Half an hour later, both the rug and her hands scrubbed spotlessly clean and yesterday's leftover stew simmering on the hob, Margaret tentatively climbed the stairs to check on the status of the toilet seat. Whilst making the herby dumplings she had heard an inordinate amount of banging and hammering but had tried to ignore it. Years of experience had taught her to be very afraid when Bob banged and hammered. Halfway across the landing, she prayed that a simple explanation would be forthcoming to account for the mounds of debris littering the dust sheets. But the scene that met her eyes as she cautiously peered round the bathroom door defied even her worst fears.

"Hello, love. Had a good day? Personally I've had better. But don't worry. I've had a word with the insurance people. You remember Steve, the one who came here on the last two occasions? Well, he popped round after I'd emailed him the pictures. When he rang back to say he was on his way, everyone was laughing.

Nice bunch in that office…"

Margaret sighed stoically. "So what happened?"

"To cut a very long story short… I don't know how I did it but I cracked the pan getting the seat off, so I had to go out and buy a new toilet. But it came with a slim-line cistern that didn't fit the space, so I had to buy some timber to box in the gap. But, would you believe it, so funny really… I put a nail through the cold water inlet!" he laughed.

Margaret's eyes narrowed. She did not laugh. She did not even smile.

"Anyway… I had to go out and buy a length of pipe. By the way, that bubble on the hall ceiling will be fine in a couple of days as long as you don't touch it. Then, and you *will* think this funny, I set fire to the blind doing the soldering and a flaming slat fell into the bath and melted a hole in it. I burnt your new oven gloves dealing with the fire so I had to throw them away. Sorry about that. I'll buy you some new ones. Anyway I took out the old bath – the new one's being delivered on Friday – but I cracked a couple of tiles in the process so I decided to take the lot off. That's when half the plaster fell off the wall. I know it looks a mess at the moment but plastering is my first job for tomorrow. And I'll mend the gaping hole in the back of your wardrobe. Sadly one or two of your work suits and a couple of your holiday dresses got a bit dusty when I inadvertently broke through with the lump hammer. So I took them to the cleaners on the way to the builder's yard. But, silly me, I forgot to drop them off first and they got covered in plaster mix when the sack fell over and split open when I went a bit too fast over the speed bump at the retail park. I'm not sure if washing them will be a good idea. They may end up looking like clothing for terracotta warriors. Ha, ha, ha… as for the exhaust… well most of it is in the gutter outside Mothercare. But you can get a couple of suits and holiday clothes in the sales. Maybe you can choose a new blind while you're at it. And I'd be ever so grateful if you could pop into the breaker's yard for an exhaust. And don't worry about the shower unit. I know it looks a bit wonky, but it'll be fine once I've tiled and grouted. But one thing I *am* certain of is that you'll love the new tiles. They've got sprigs of lavender on them…"

Margaret stood in stunned silence, too shocked even to laugh hysterically.

When the power of speech finally returned, she mumbled weakly, "I'm going to Dad's."

*

With the container of beef stew and dumplings in a shopping bag in one hand and a bunch of keys that would embarrass a gaoler at the Tower of London in the other, a dazed Margaret set off towards the warden-controlled flats at the bottom of the road. Before reaching the entrance, she stopped, sighed loudly and gazed up at the starry heavens.

"Are you having a laugh?" she hissed vehemently, much to the consternation of a couple of lads walking past.

"We never said nuffink, Missus."

"How long do you think I will put up with this?" she continued, wagging her finger. "I want this to stop right now. Understand?"

"Sorry, Missus," the teenagers muttered, although neither had the faintest idea what they were apologising for or who this crazy woman was. But she sounded really mad, or drunk, or both, and her shopping bag was giving off smoke... best to humour her and disappear. Quickly.

Once inside her father's medium dependency block – named Brad Pitt House following a poll of the residents in which only Mrs Cartwright had bothered to vote on renaming the unit and, rules being rules in a democracy, the majority decision had won – Margaret made her way to her father's flat and opened the door.

"Meals on wheels!" she called in her cheeriest of voices.

But he wasn't in his living room and the bedroom was empty.

Margaret walked to the communal lounge where a lone Mrs Cartwright was watching *Fight Club*. She then sped off to the warden's office with 90-year-old Mrs Cartwright hard on her heels. When sensing a bit of excitement, Mrs Cartwright could really motor.

"Don't worry," Lyn explained. "Monday night is supper club night."

"Since when?" Margaret demanded.

"Since today. Oh, did you not get the email?"

"Perhaps. I haven't opened my emails," Margaret replied.

"That's because the first rule of supper club is that you never talk about supper club," Mrs Cartwright commented solemnly. Then she cackled like the Wicked Witch of the West before returning to her beloved Brad who was on pause in the lounge.

"Your dad's at The George," Lyn continued. "They do a really good beef stew and dumplings. I believe that's his favourite dinner, isn't it?"

Margaret flew down the corridor to her father's flat, picked up the stew, slammed the door behind her and strode purposefully outside – much to the consternation of the same two lads who were attempting to break into a clapped-out Astra. They ran off the moment they caught sight of this mad woman who looked even crazier than before.

She crashed into her house, sloshed the stew and dumplings into a clean bowl, stamped upstairs and unceremoniously shoved it into Bob's hand.

"Robert Phillips... You will not leave this bathroom until it is finished to my satisfaction. And if you botch it, I will call in a professional and hand over all the money you have earmarked for that home cinema set-up that will allow you to watch sport all day and every day in High Definition!"

"Don't get into such a tizzy, Maggie. You'll see the funny side of this in the morning. Honest you will," he soothed, putting his arm around her shoulder.

"Take. Your. Hands. Off. Me!" she hissed through gritted teeth before inhaling deeply to regain her composure. "I am now going to my room to pack a bag," she announced calmly. "I shall stay in the spa hotel at Crossways until the bathroom is finished. Don't forget to feed Dad and the cat. And if either of them is sick, then clean it up! And, by the way ... I hate lavender!"

9.45pm

With a flute of champagne in her hand, Margaret luxuriated in bergamot-scented bubbles. A near-empty bottle stood on the marble floor next to the half-finished box of Charbonnel et Walker fondants. All the knots had been teased out of her back and neck by the gentle hands of Michael, who had commented that never in his life had he come across anyone quite as tense. Did she lead a stressful life?

After taking another sip of champagne, Margaret decided that she would book in for one Saturday night each month despite the cost. Bob would cope admirably for 36 hours without her. He would buy fish and chips for him and Dad for Saturday lunch followed by hours of football on the home cinema in the newly-decorated back bedroom courtesy of the new pasting table. They would have cheese on toast and a bowl of Heinz tomato soup during football round-up. And on Sunday, after lunch at the British Legion, they would watch even more football. Or rugby. Or golf. Or Formula One. But never tennis.

She knew Bob would be a little nervous without her. Not that he suffered from separation anxiety or anything like that. It was just that she was the voice of reason that talked him out of another DIY project that would invariably go wrong and over budget. Exactly how much did a 35 pound toilet seat end up costing? 500 pounds in insurance excess, a couple of work suits, some holiday clothes and a car exhaust.

*

As she lay in bed watching back-to-back episodes of Pride and Prejudice, and after leaving a message for Mr Upjohn to say she would not be in work the following day – her first day sick in over 30 years, so she had to be suffering from dengue fever or the plague – she felt a twinge of guilt. But only a tiny twinge...

~

Sue Powis' Biography

Born in Birmingham and resident of Solihull for more than 30 years. Mother of two children. Taught in Birmingham schools for many years eventually specialising in Special Needs. Assistant in Speech and Language Therapy in Solihull PCT for young adults with Downs Syndrome.

Photographic volunteer for The War Graves Photographic Project, an arm of The Commonwealth War Graves Commission.

Written many articles in various magazines concerning my work for the War Graves Commission.

OWN DEVICES

Shortlisted story, by Will Ingrams

"Yeah, no, ya right, Desky. You way mo' pow'ful 'n me man, way more. You got dat big ole processor, man, and all dat bayspace, right? You prob'ly do borin' stuff real fast, doncha, but dat don' make you smart, man. It's me dat's smart, 'cause I'm up to date, see? Trendin' man."

"But I'm afraid that doesn't make sense to me at all, Mister Tab – that is what I'm supposed to call you, isn't it? OK. The way I see things, you're more of an entertainer, you see. No, don't take offence, Mister Tab, I'm not trivialising you and your functions; people need to unwind sometimes, and you clearly have your role to play, but for serious work, for the spreadsheets and reports, they still need a proper desktop like me. So I would still be the smart choice for the important things, don't you see?"

"No man, I don't! You so ol' fashion, Desky. OK so you got ya Bluetooth nah, overwise we couldn' be talkin' right? But dat's only there really fo' yo' keyboard connection, man. An' who needs one o' dem dese days? Look at me, man. I got GPS, so I always know where I am. I got touch, so I'm, like, really sensitive, at one wiv de user, an' I can magic de keyboard up, if ya really need it, in ma software man. No hassle. An' the killer is, Desky, I don' gotta be plugged in all de time. So I'm there forever like, part of life, de constant companion. Dat's what it's about now, Desky. On de move, in touch, always ready, get it done, man, wherever you is, right?"

"Excuse me buttin' in, guys, but you're takin' up a wee bit o' bandwidth here, and I cannae get through to our new colleague, Nik. Could ye no gie it a rest?"

"Oh, shut it McPrinty! You're like out o' the Ark, sis, you know dat? Ink on paper? That's like so old, so faded, y'know. An' bad fo' the 'viroment, too, sis. Dat's trees you usin' y'know. Choppin' down trees. Look, anyone can read da news now, read books, read anything right off my screen, like just anywhere, yeah? No printin'!"

"Now, now, Mister Tab, there's absolutely no call for rudeness, you know. McPrinty's been here rather longer than you, and she does valuable hard copy work, as well as scanning images for both of us, after all. Have a little respect please."

"Respec' what man? I don' need help wi' no scannin' – I got cameras, I got OCR, I got image editin' all built in, guys! An' people don' need no printouts no more – you jus' take me wid you. S'all onscreen man! S'portable."

"Hey buddies, lighten up! Let me introduce myself to y'all, huh? They call me Nik and I'm gonna be working with all of you guys, right, so we need a little give and take here, OK? Look, Mister Tab, I know you got a built-in camera, yeah OK, OK, two cameras, but come on, Tabby, you gotta admit they're both pieces of shit, right? You might have eight megapixels on paper – sorry, make that 'in theory' – but your itsy bitsy little plastic lenses couldn't resolve the petals on a frickin' daisy! I got real multi-element zoom lenses and I can open up all the way to F1.8 so, hey, I could separate a gnat's balls by candlelight, right? Now look, I'm gonna need to communicate with ol' Desky here for the Photoshop stuff, OK? And I'm not counting you out, Mister Tab, 'cause I know you're gonna be just fantastic for checkin' out the shots on location – I can talk Bluetooth to you or we can share the SD, buddy. But I also get to bypass both of you guys if I need to – I can talk sweet to lil ol' McPrinty herself, y'know, and we don't need no wires. And I'm surely lookin' forward to that Miss Mac."

"Yeah right! Das all we need, anuvva know-it-all accessory on da scene, takin' up de commoonicashun channels wiv his big aperture, innit? An' how come you talkin' like dat man? I bet you really from da far east, just like da rest of us, yeah?"

"Look buddy, you can't argue with global manufacturing. It's true that most of my components originate across the Pacific, but you can bet your sweet ass-embly that I'm tailored to the big ol' US market. It's just good luck for y'all that I'm over here."

"Over-specced, over-priced and not wanted over here, das what I fink. Who needs a heavy ole camera dese days, huh? Dis da worlda Instagram, man, not family portraits."

"Now there's no call to be uncivil, Mister Tab. Clearly someone in the family intends to take high quality photographs with Nik here, and they will need us all to talk properly to each other for efficient processing. Protocol and handshakes all round, please."

"Well I, for one, like your style, Nik, any road up. Your data stream can flow into my loch any day; we'll enjoy being paired. But I'll tell you guys somethin' else that's new. I've been scannin' the waves and just logged a web-wise television in the house. Says she's smart, wide and high in all the appropriate places."

"What dey get dat for? I can do TV y'know; dey should be gettin' rid o' the telly not buyin' a new one."

"Just my point, Mister Tab. I know you can do all sorts of things on a personal and portable level, but sometimes people want to watch a bigger screen, something fixed and functional, like a proper desktop, or a big family television."

"Hey guys, if this new TV has wireless, we can all talk to her, right? I could display my pictures for the whole family, and Mister Tab, you can send YouTube stuff to her, huh buddy?"

"Yeah man, dat's cool. Fink it's gonna leave Desky further out in da cold though, eh?"

"I beg to differ. Anyway, my tablet friend, you should be more worried about our absent colleague Moby, don't you think? He can do all the things that you can, and he's more portable than you – gets taken out all the time. A real personal assistant, I'd say. That's why he's not in on our little wireless chat – he's off being useful to people."

"But he's got a tiny screen, man, you don' wanna do yo' email on dat. It's gonna do yer eyes in pretty damn quick, innit? An' sorry guys, but I fink Nik here ain't never gonna get a chance to chat to our Moby, is he? 'Cause once they get dat new TV workin' proper, I fink Moby's gonna become a little remote. A little remote, geddit?"

"Och, too corny, Mister Tab. Hey, I can sense a wee problem here though – looks like someone's downloading a power management App onto Moby. So even when they're miles away, they can turn off the wifi and the..."

~

Will Ingrams' Biography

Will was born in London but grew up in Hampshire before studying Physics in Manchester. He has taught a range of subjects to children and adults in both the UK and the Caribbean, and has also worked in the computing industry. Will began to devote more time to fiction writing in 2011, experimenting with form and style. He was successful in reaching the long-list for the 2014 Bristol Short Story Prize, and is a member of Stradbroke BigSky Writers. He lives in rural Suffolk with his wife and family.

Will's site: www.willingwordwhirl.wordpress.com

PSEUDONYM

Shortlisted story, by Richard Dunford

That letter arrives in the post.

That letter you've received a thousand times before.

That letter you half want to just chuck straight in the bin.

That letter with those oh so familiar words... only this time, those words are missing. They've been replaced with new words.

These new words are alien.

You have to read it three times over.

You have to slap cold water in your face to check you're not dreaming.

You've applied to funding schemes to turn your passion projects into reality so many times the rejection just bounces off you like a sponge.

We thank you for taking the time to submit your proposal but unfortunately on this occasion we won't be recommending you for arts funding.

You've read it so many times.

They always encourage you to submit further work in the future. I guess this covers all their bases. Your next submission could end up a masterpiece that defines a generation.

Tactical sympathetic disappointment is the order of the day.

It's not right for us, or, *this isn't quite the direction we're going in at the moment*, is not the damnation that you haven't an ounce of talent in your pathetic soul.

It's not the harsh dose of reality that will be ringing in your ears as you take a walk up to the roof of the tallest building you can find and step off the ledge.

Where are those familiar words?!

Where's the template rejection letter and the hollow best wishes for all your future endeavours?

Don't give up. We don't want the guilt of your spiral into a lifetime condemned to dead end minimum wage jobs on our conscience.

But when that letter arrives with new words you've never seen before. Words like 'acceptance'.

'Congratulations'. 'Approved'. 'Granted'.

A sentence that begins with, *We're delighted to inform you...*

Well, you'll tell the interviewer in the retrospective documentary on your ascent to superstardom that you took it in your stride... but you know otherwise.

You know you did a silly dance.

You know you ran around the house screaming like a schoolgirl hyped up on fizzy drinks.

It's the greatest moment of your life.

All those art classes.

All those late nights.

All the double shifts stacking shelves in budget supermarkets to buy brushes, canvases and an easel that didn't collapse every two hours.

All the times you struggled to get the paint clean from underneath your fingernails and watched a rainbow of colours rinse down the plughole.

Suddenly it's all worth it.

And then in the blink of an eye the rug gets pulled out from under you.

There and then is when you remember.

You remember what you did.

You remember the form.

That bloody equal opportunities monitoring form.

You'd spent hours crafting applications before. Poured your heart and soul onto that page only to feel it sink once you reached the end and had to fill out the mandatory equal opportunities form.

They always say this form has no bearing on your application.

So why are you asking then?!

You were a heterosexual white male.

The epitome of the majority.

As soon as you ticked those boxes you might as well have erased every word that had come before.

Just once you think, *what the heck.*

Just once you bend the rules.

You have this theory they have to give finance to certain criteria to appease the government and look fair, so just this once… you go wild.

Problem is, the one time you weren't completely honest with your application and told a couple of little white lies is the one time you get asked in for an interview.

Get asked to attend the contract signing in person.

Get asked to take publicity photos as you sign on the dotted line.

Get asked to make a personal appearance in front of the board of directors before the funding for your new art exhibition gets transferred into your bank account.

A bank account you now have to set up in a pseudonym as you couldn't use your real name for the application as that name had applied multiple times already.

Trouble is they're not expecting a heterosexual white male to walk through those doors.

The people who can change your life forever and finally give you the funding to take your work to the next level... they're expecting a transgender bisexual from an ethnic minority with a disability to enter that room.

You know it's wrong but you don't want to wave goodbye to that money.

You know it's wrong but you grow a beard and dress up like a drag queen.

You know it's wrong but you paint your own skin and practice an accent.

You know it's wrong but you buy a wheelchair off eBay and inject your legs with a sedative just in case you lose concentration at the interview.

You know it's wrong but this is the opportunity you've been waiting for your whole lifetime.

And when you get in front of that board of directors the last person in the world you wanted to see is sitting centre stage.

The one you dated through university.

The one you sat up late with night after night talking about how together you'd take the art world by storm.

The one who knows you better than anyone on the planet.

The one you insisted was the most beautiful girl you'd ever seen so she'd give you a blow job even though she'd told you the thought of performing oral sex made her stomach churn.

The one you gave the boot after the chick who you really thought was the most beautiful girl in the world gave you her number when you flirted outside a local takeaway.

That one. She's staring right into your lying, deceitful eyes as you try and convince the board you're disabled, from an ethnic minority and in the middle of a sex change.

You know she knows who you are.

You know she knows you're a big fat liar.

You know any moment she'll expose you.

Any moment you're gonna officially be the worst human being alive and hated by each and every minority you've exploited for your own selfish gain.

For a moment you think to yourself, *If only I'd stuck with her maybe she'd have got me the funding I longed for*.

Maybe you could offer to lick her out in return for some decent paints and a work space to develop new ideas.

You wait for that moment... but it never comes.

For some reason she keeps silent.

For some reason she lets you pull off the pretence.

For some reason she lets you sign on that dotted line.

And finally you've won. Finally you have the money

you've always needed to dedicate your life to your art.

Before you know it your face is in magazines.

Before you know it your work's revered by collectors around the world.

Before you know it those original paintings you would've sold for a week's rent are being fought over at auction and going for seven figures.

Before you know it you're a household name... only it's not your name.

It's your pseudonym.

Paranoid you'll get discovered you get your skin permanently bleached and book in for the sex change operation.

Paranoid you'll get caught out you pay a homeless drunk to cripple your legs with a baseball bat.

Paranoid your whole world will come crumbling down you hire a hitman to take out the one person who knows the truth.

As the years go by you forget your real name altogether.

You embrace the pseudonym.

You become the pseudonym.

You become a living breathing piece of art.

And you paint.

It's the life you've always wanted.

So it didn't go quite how you originally imagined.

So you had to tell a few white lies to get where you needed to be.

You said you'd do anything to live your dreams... and you meant it.

~

Richard Dunford's Biography

Writer and filmmaker from the south coast of England. Debut novel *TABULA RASA* published by new dawn publishers in 2012 (available on Amazon). Debut no budget feature as writer/director *POV* due to be completed 2014.

Richard on IMDB:
www.imdb.com/name/nm4705281/

RELUCTANT HEROES

Shortlisted story, by John Emms

"I've got it. It's phone-boxes, isn't it?" Angela clapped her hands in delight. "You don't like walking past phone-boxes."

Her pleasure at working out why Steve was taking her on such a roundabout route to the café was palpable. They had met at the station, bumping into each other as they got off the same train and the attraction had been instant. Steve had suggested going for a coffee, but his habit of stopping at every junction to look down each street before deciding which to take had intrigued her.

"Am I right?"

"No... yes... look, let's just find a coffee shop first."

Eventually, and apparently by random chance (it was surprising how many phone boxes there still were, despite the ubiquitous mobiles), they found a Starbucks and purchased two bucket-sized mugs of, judging by the price, lukewarm liquid gold.

Sitting down, Steve stared into his coffee.

"You see, it's difficult to explain..."

"Is it that you're afraid they'll ring as you pass and you'll have to answer?"

"No, no, it's not that."

"Do you think someone might jump out at you?"

"No, of course not... quite the opposite in fact."

"The opposite?"

"I have to go inside. I can't get past phone-boxes without going in."

"Going in? But why?"

"I don't know. It started a few years ago. On my 18th birthday, as it happens. It got so bad I had to move out of town and live in the country. There aren't so many of them there. And I know where they all are. But I had to come into town today for some business."

"Golly. How odd. So, when you go in – what happens? Do you call someone?"

"No. No, I don't. I... well, something happens to me."

"Happens?" Angela's eyes widened. "Do you mean, like, well... you know?"

"No, no – nothing like that. No, it's just that, well, all my muscles seem to, well – expand, you know? And I sort of burst out of my clothes and I'm standing there in this ridiculous coloured suit with a huge B on my chest and these really indelicate tights."

"Tights?"

"Yeah, tights. And when I come out of the phone-box people start running around shouting 'Gee!' and 'Wow!' and 'Hey, look, guys, it's Big Boy!' And then some stupid girl is always screaming and there'll be some bizarre person trying to abduct her and she'll see me and screech 'Save me, Big Boy, save me!' So I'll have to save her and then everyone crowds round and it's so embarrassing I have to stick one fist up in the air and rocket up into the sky to get away and often enough the stupid girl is still attached to me and I have no idea what to do with her and I don't know where to go and anyway by then I've usually forgotten what I was doing before the phone-box got me."

Angela took a drink of coffee, staring at him.

"That does sound rather inconvenient," she said.

"Too bloody right."

They looked at each other, then Angela looked away.

"You know," she said, "I have a similar sort of problem."

"You do?"

"Mhm."

"What – phone boxes?"

"No, no. Phone boxes would be easy."

"You think so, do you?"

"You can avoid phone-boxes. As you've shown."

"Not always."

"Oh? Well, anyway – my problem is people."

"People?"

"Not just any people. People with problems. Or under threat. Who need protection. Things you can't see by looking at them."

"Like my stupid girls?"

"Not really, no. It's difficult to explain."

"That's what I said. But I managed to tell you."

"Yes, well... all right, then. It's people who need a guardian angel."

"A what?" Steve inadvertently splashed about a pound's worth of coffee onto the table.

"A guardian angel."

"You mean like Clarence in that film – *It's a Wonderful Life*."

"Not exactly. Well, perhaps. A bit." She paused, then leaned forward. "Would you like to look down my jumper?"

"What? Oh! Yes, please!" He reached towards her.

"No! Down the back."

"Oh. Sorry."

Getting up and moving behind her, he pulled her jumper from the back of her neck and looked inside. At first he wasn't sure what he was seeing, but then his mind focused.

There, tightly furled and pressed against her back, was a pair of beautiful white wings.

~

John Emms' Biography

A few years ago I retired from a career as a local government lawyer, during which the only vaguely creative writing I could manage was for professional journals, so not wildly exciting. I now at last have the time to indulge my long-held desire to write in a way which is less vaguely creative, with a number of short stories and articles published here and there, not least in *Slightly Foxed* and *The Oldie*, though rather a lot not published anywhere. I have also written a few plays, only one of which has been performed and won prizes.

SONNY'S JULIET

Shortlisted story, by Tom Norton

"The moon," she said, leaning into him so they touched from shoulder to elbow. "It's up there just for us."

What bollocks, Sonny thought, before confirming his agreement. Alone in the dark stairwell, leaning on a narrow windowsill, he pressed his upper arm firmly against hers. Her smell was overwhelming. It didn't seem like perfume though; not any perfume he'd detected on girls before. Fisher told him about pheromones once: was that this? Could you *smell* pheromones? He liked the idea of Amy Green's body calling to him unconsciously, against her better judgement. But *she* had leant into *him,* and when he pressed back she remained; and it was hot there, where they touched through the fabric of their outfits.

A loud thud and a scream drifted to them through the double doors, followed by a low ripple of laughter. They had two or three minutes here together, before he had to go. She stood against him in silence, her head slightly turned, as though regarding his reflection in the glass. Was she waiting for him to do something? Why did it have to be *him?* The butterflies inside him all evening had turned into birds; or bats. Massive vampire bats.

With a sigh she dropped her head onto his shoulder and shuffled her face against his neck. The bats broke through his stomach lining, battered into his heart, then beat a pulsing path downwards, to where he already pressed himself hard against the wall.

The muffled laughter from beyond the doors, the moon that was there just for them, the overpowering haze of pheromones, the fact he was perhaps 85% confident of his lines, the almost certain knowledge he was going to suffer a heart attack at the tender age of 15: these dreadful things conspired to have him turn his upper body to her, position an arm around her wonderful waist and kiss her open, painted mouth.

"Oi, dickhead!" A voice whispered urgently from the stairs. "You're on!"

Bradley Shaw, the giant backstage runner from Year 11 who was too dim and volatile to get a proper part, looked at them both, his delighted smirk confirming that their secret was very far from safe. He had a palm against the double doors and started beckoning furiously.

Suddenly mortified, Sonny moved away from the wall, and as she unhooked herself from him, her forearm brushed against the stick of rock within his trousers. Her eyes widened and met his own.

"Just... give me a minute," he mumbled in terror to Bradley, "...sort myself out."

When Shaw's eyes lit up in realisation, they instantly filled with the most malicious of mischief. Grinning wildly, he grabbed Sonny with a chubby paw, burst open the door to the hall and thrust him roughly into the lights. The sheer momentum of the shove took him to the top of the makeshift ramp constructed by the stage, on which he stood bow-legged, hands clasped within his costume shop trousers, looking down upon the grey, silent faces of his parents, who sat in the front row. Hunched and blinking in the lights, he was aware of the lipstick all around his mouth and smeared across one cheek. Towards the back, past the pool of darkly-clad parents, it was easy to distinguish the rows of white shirts belonging to perhaps 40 of his colleagues at St. Martin's.

By the time he had staggered his way across the stage, past the horrified face of Mr McRae, all lit up behind the curtain by his little prompting lamp, the crowd's nervous laughter had descended into wolf whistles and ironic cheers.

*

Sonny had not visited many hospitals in his time. He had never broken anything, never consumed cleaning products as a child, and had never had cause to visit dying relatives. Until today. Grandad Wally had been taken in the weekend before the play, another reason why Sonny's onstage mishap had been taken as a personal affront by his mother, who 'didn't need all this right now.' The heart attack occurred during the credits of the *Casualty* series finale, and Nanny Babs, accustomed to his humour after 50 years of marriage, assumed her husband's collapse was a theatrical commentary on the quality of the acting in her favourite Saturday-night show. It wasn't until she had resolutely made two cups of tea that she had noticed the drool on the carpet and rushed to phone an ambulance.

Now Grandad Wally lay propped up by hospital pillows, semi-conscious and, as Sonny's father put it, 'on the way out.' Sonny regarded him through the window before slowly pushing open the door to the ward. His mother rose from the bedside and approached, her eyes now dry after a day of tears.

"Sonny," she whispered. "How was today?"

He blushed furiously, his humiliation returning in a wave. Today his climbing social stature seemed to have taken a permanent nosedive. The number of times the word 'boner' was directed at him during the 15 minutes of morning registration was surely worthy of record in the Yearbook, and things had gone downhill from there. To make matters worse, Amy had not come in to school. All day Sonny remorsefully imagined her at home, too embarrassed by their episode to face the taunts and jibes from the bullies and the people she called friends, tears of injustice falling to her pink pillows at being denied the chance to absorb the just and proper praise for her performance, and dispelling the name Sonny Miller from her as though spitting out a mouldy piece of bread.

"I'm sorry I shouted," his mother continued, looking

at him intently. "Things'll clear up, you'll see. They'll all forget."

"No, they won't," was his almost inaudible reply. Almost to change the subject he nodded to the bed. "Is he any better, Mum?"

She was silent, her eyes drifting away from him. "I think it's important that you see him now. Talk to him. He'll know your voice."

Amid the greenish curtains and whitish medical equipment, his grandad's mouth hung open, the large grey head moving almost imperceptibly from side to side. "I'll wait on the seats through there. Do you want a drink or anything?"

He didn't. He wanted to get on with this. His mother left him to settle onto a hard plastic chair. "Hello Gangan," he said, immediately feeling embarrassed at using the childish name. "Hello Grandad. It's me: James. Sonny." The old man was unresponsive: this wasn't going very well. Should he carry on? What on earth does he talk about? He fiddled with the zip of his jacket, watching the grey head rock slowly in the pillows.

"There's this girl, Grandad," he began, eventually. "Her name's Amy. She's got brown hair and beautiful dark eyes. I think I like her. I mean, I do like her; a *lot.* Yesterday, we kissed each other; she wanted me to kiss her so I did. I've never really felt like this before, Grandad. For ages, when I've been talking to her I've felt like I want to be sick, or jump up and down or something; just shout out as loud as I can, like I've got this energy in me that I need to get out."

All of a sudden, Sonny stopped. His grandfather's lips were moving amidst the white bristles of his beard. Listening closely, words could be heard carried on his breath. Then Sonny realised that the old man wasn't talking but singing, and the lines were from a song before his time:

"...don't mind the grey skies...you'll make 'em blue, Sonny Boy..."

And Sonny knew the song. He had heard it many times before, but during childhood; during another life entirely it seemed. He would sit at the feet of a tatty brown armchair, climbing Lego men up its flanks and onto its soft arms, jumping them to knees in grey pinstripe trousers. Around him would drift the soft voice of his Grandad Wally; always the same song, always choking on the same lines – "I still have you, Sonny Boy" – and when the song stopped Sonny would see tears streaming freely down the old man's face, his head held still as stone toward the window, not looking there at all but miles beyond; to an unreachable place, full of loss and grief and regret.

"James!" his mother's voice would call him through the doorway. Grandad Wally would look across and smile as though no tears at all were in his eyes.

"Off you go, Sonny," he would say, "Go and help your mother."

*

The next day was a Thursday, and for Sonny Thursdays signified one thing: Double Graphics. Agonisingly poised after lunch, the hour and 40 minutes of group project work with Amy Green usually filled his morning with a kind of breathless anxiety, which, if he embraced and channelled correctly, could become the most exhilarating way to deal with the stifling tedium of Mr Banks's moustachioed maths and Mr Clancy's bearded geography. On this particular Thursday, however, the presence of Amy on the day's horizon hung like the very Sword of Damocles above his poor young head.

That morning he had seen her unmistakable figure across the playground, walking with two of her girlfriends, who interlocked their arms in a firm display of their allegiance. He had turned and hurried off in the opposite direction: a lion pit was not the place for their first encounter. It would be graphics; it would be their CD album cover and promotional poster campaign. They would laugh through it all together; things were going to turn out OK. However, fate was to take the form of the school Secretary, who pulled him out of Geography, loudly announcing that his mum was on the phone, much to the grinning delight of his classmates.

"Sonny," his mother's voice said quietly, "I've talked with the school. Get a bus and wait for us at the hospital. He's got worse."

So there he sat in the battered bus stop outside the school, double graphics fully underway. Glaring out across the street he thought of Amy, trying to concentrate on their project alone, tucking hair behind her ear the way she did. He saw Grandad Wally's bewildered face moving from side to side within the grey pillows. Then out of nowhere his grandfather was grinning, throwing his arms up in the air, a tennis ball clasped in one hand; and Sonny was laughing too, their eyes connected in a moment of joy; his feet sinking in the sand where he had bowled the spinning ball to undo his father's stubborn batting, and the sound of waves were crashing all around. And he felt something spilling upwards from inside; a sadness rising too fast like shaken up Coca-Cola, and he knew it was going to overspill and there was nothing he could do to stop it.

"Are you alright, Sonny?" His heart plummeted like a

depth charge at the sound of the voice. Of all the people, of all the times, it was Amy Green who joined him in the bus stop.

"You got off early," he managed to say.

"We're flying to Barbados tonight."

"That's good." Sonny's parents never flew him anywhere, and would never dream of doing so a week before the end of term.

"Are you alright?" she said again. Looking sidelong at his welling eyes, her expression was an odd mix of guilt and embarrassment, and he felt an urgent need to clarify that she, and their 'incident', had no relation to his tears.

"It's... my grandad," he said with difficulty. "He's on the way... he's going to... die." All at once, the nauseous emotion grabbed him fully and his sobbing body leant forward in his lap, face hidden shamefully in folded arms. He felt her hand slide within his and he clasped at it instinctively.

"Sorry," he kept saying, "I'm sorry," and then her head was pressed against him, soft hair on his cheek, her lips there against his neck again.

"Shh... don't talk. Don't try to fight against it... sometimes it's the best thing."

In the corner of his eye, he saw the blue and orange of the 21 appear; and he knew how little he wanted this excruciatingly magnificent moment to end. He half turned to her, but she seemed to read his thoughts and smiled. "I can get this one," she gave his hand a squeeze. "Come on."

The fat driver regarded Sonny's blotchy face with barely disguised amusement, but the bus was empty enough and they managed to claim the front seat on the upper deck. The road was clear and quiet before the mania of the school run and Sonny felt calmer now, privileged to be sitting beside her; to have her to himself.

"I thought you were great," he said after a while; then felt himself flush. "As Juliet, I mean."

"Thanks." Her awkward smile was reassuring.

At the traffic lights they saw Mrs Levine, the expression of timid panic eternally on her face, mounting her bicycle like a frail twig. She noticed them on the bus and, terrified, smiled up at them. Sonny hid a wanking gesture beneath the bus's parapet, and the two of them disguised their hysterics by grinning their greetings broadly back. Rolling into town they entertained each other by pointing out the weirdoes, the nutters and the fogies, who were out in force at this time of day. One old woman's head was pushed so far forward it was a marvel she could see where she was going, and Sonny did an impression. Amy struggled for breath and almost fell out of the seat. He had never felt happier and they sat in easy silence, swaying in unison to the rock and swell of the bus.

It was as they turned onto the High Street that she asked him: "Do you ever look at people, Sonny?"

"Look at people?"

"Ever look at them and think, 'what's happening now for that person?'"

"Er–"

"It's like – that guy over there. We can see him and everything around him; but he sees it all from a different angle. He experiences it all in a completely different way. *I'm* seeing things differently now, from *you*. It's like everyone we're looking at has a bubble around their head – a mist. And in that mist is that person's own thoughts; and they'll never be the same as anybody else's."

Sonny was starting to feel uncomfortable, but she was animated and carried on. "The world seems the same for everyone, but it isn't. There are millions of different worlds; and not one of them is the same. It's something my dad says. Look down the street: see the mist round everyone's head – like a helmet in a spacesuit – full of their own thoughts and memories.

"And them over there," she pointed earnestly. "Their bubbles are connecting: certain things they're saying mean something to both of them – but they've got no idea how the other one is seeing things."

She turned, and it was clearly the look on his face that made her falter. It was the only time he had ever seen her blush.

"It's just..." she flapped her arms, "I can't explain it. It's just – *interesting*." She was desperate now, looking about her through the windows and shifting in discomfort. Eventually, she settled upright in the seat, holding her face straight ahead, and his heart hammered through a lengthy pause. Then, quietly – excruciatingly – she apologised.

Sonny's heart sank, slowly, like a dinner plate submerging in a soapy sink.

"No," he said, leaning forward, his voice an unconvincing whine. "No, I think I know what you mean." He looked intently at a couple by the bus stop. "The mist."

But it was far too late, and they reached the bottom of the hill in a silence hot with embarrassment. The stillness tautened and stretched, and he was painfully aware that he should find something to say. Eventually, she leant forward, rummaging for something in her bag, and he studied the way her dark hair fell against her thighs. He could see the black bra-strap through the pressed white of her blouse, and he felt a familiar dry lump in his throat.

She straightened again, and hit the button to stop the bus before scribbling something on a scrap of orange paper. "You know," she said, "if you want to hang out in the summer. I'm away for two weeks, but call me then; if you want to."

He looked at the number and was gripped by a sudden, inexplicable urge to cry. *Don't,* he told himself furiously. *For God's sake, just don't!*

She stood and gripped the handrail as the bus began to slow, looking down at him with a sad little smile. He tried to speak but his mouth seemed dusty and parched.

"Have a nice summer, Sonny" she said.

He swivelled in the seat and watched as she made her way down the stairs, working against the sharp braking of the bus. *Do it, Sonny: tell her now*. "Amy," he called, but the voice whispered out of him, evaporating between them as her dark head disappeared.

His eyes lingered on the empty stairwell then he raised them to see an elderly couple watching him from the sunlight. The old man was smiling and there was moisture in his quiet eyes.

Sonny turned awkwardly to fold the scrap of paper into a pocket of his trousers.

*

In the ward Sonny settled himself glumly in the plastic seat, where he sat and listened to the beeps of the machine, waiting for his family to arrive. With each skip of the little green line across the monitor he thought of

Amy, disappearing down the stairwell, flying to Barbados, slipping through his fingers.

After a while, he reached for a framed photograph that had been added to the bedside since his previous visit. Sonny recognised it from the bookshelf in his living room. It showed four people and a dark-coloured car, with long grass, sand, and a grey sea visible in the distance. His mother was there: no older than he was now; eyes narrowed against the sun, grinning and holding a hand to her blustering hair. Nanny Babs leant in at her side, mouth open conspiratorially to her daughter, a familiar sparkle in her eyes. A beaming Grandad Wally leant back on the frame of the car, arm clasped around the narrow shoulders of the fourth figure, a young boy, who was more of a mystery to Sonny. The boy held a shy, excited smile; suggesting that the holiday, the photograph, perhaps his father's embrace, were rare events. Sonny knew who it was, of course: it was Uncle Stan. But this person wasn't real to him: only the subject of rare and uncomfortable conversations; stunted, unsatisfactory stories, which were always brought to an end by a hardening of his mother's face. Sonny realised he had never *really* looked at pictures of his uncle; never taken him in. But here, amongst the unfriendly sterility of the ward, he examined the boy's face, astounded. It was a face he knew so well; intimately, in fact; a face he looked at every single day.

"Unbelievable," he said.

Suddenly, his grandad spluttered and Sonny let the picture clatter to the floor. Kicking back the chair, he stood bolt upright at the side of the bed. The large grey head rocked forward then pushed back hard into the pillow, turning red, a piece of vomit dribbling from the mouth.

Sonny was motionless, heart racing, body waiting numbly for the brain's instructions. A shrill ringing in his head dampened any thought process he put in place and it took an almost physical effort to override the blankness. The piercing noise, he discovered, was coming from the equipment. "Help," he croaked. The old man's gasping face had turned crimson within the white and grey bristles.

Sonny watched as the ward around him shifted and the bed approached; the pained old face came closer. He heard his own voice ring clearly around the ward: "For fuck's sake: Nurse! Someone!" He saw his hand extend to pull a tissue from a box and wipe the mouth and bearded chin; then there he sat, on the bed, hands upon his grandad's shoulders, looking down upon his face.

The wrinkled eyelids flickered open and the soft blue eyes moved about in panicked bursts, adjusting to the light. Then they settled on his own and widened in sheer bewilderment. When the voice came it was quiet, clear, and filled with hope.

"Stanley?"

Sonny was very close to correcting him: the words had gathered in his head and were forming in his mouth – *No, Gan-gan, it's me: Sonny* – but the bemused anticipation, the eagerness on the old man's face, choked the words before he spoke. Then, staring down into the quickly clouding eyes, into the mist that gathered round the big grey head, Sonny remembered in a wave; and he knew what he must do.

"Yes," he said, bold and soft. "It's Stanley. I'm right here, Dad. It's me. I'm here now."

Half a lifetime of sorrow lifted from Wallace

Browne's bewildered face, and Sonny watched the smile that spread, blissful and pure, across its bearded breadth. The image of a young boy's face, one that had been lost for 30 years, was forever printed on the old man's eyes, and as they closed he whispered, "Stanley, son; my sonny boy," and his head settled gently back into the pillows.

Sonny felt hands on his back. He allowed them to remove him from the bed and shepherd him towards the curtain, from where he looked on. His fingers found their way to grip the scrap of orange paper in his pocket. *Do you ever look at people, Sonny?* There were noises all around him now: urgent voices and machinery; but he listened only to the melodic murmurs of his grandad, as he drifted away. The old man's voice swam into his head, amplified by memories as clear as ice. And there was music too: a harmony for the whispered words of a song before his time.

~

Tom Norton's Biography

Tom Norton is a freelance writer with a growing collection of short stories and flash fiction that have appeared in various anthologies. Spending his day job writing strategic planning reports for university management, his mind unsurprisingly itches for more exciting, fantastical worlds. He spends his evenings studying for Birkbeck's MA in Creative Writing, and has a novel in the early stages of its long journey to completion.

THE BALLAD OF BILLY-BOB

Shortlisted story, by Andrew Campbell-Kearsey

"I wanna thank y'all for coming out to see me play this evenin'. It's mighty humblin' for a plain-speakin' country boy like me to be surrounded by so many good folk and feel all that lovin'."

He stooped to pick up yet another bunch of red roses that a fan had thrown onto the stage. His first breakthrough, million-selling hit had been entitled 'The Red Rose of Mississippi'. The crowd knew he'd complete his encore with that song. He put his hand on the top of his head to ensure that his Stetson didn't slip out of place.

He stood in front of the microphone, clutching the

bouquet as he sang his signature tune. In fanzines he was quoted as saying, "Cut me down the middle and you'll see Country and Western music running right through me." He'd claimed that the lyrics of this song were terribly personal and he often hinted at them being autobiographical. There wasn't a dry eye in the hall as he sang of a boy growing up in a trailer park in Tennessee. In the first verse he loses his Mama when she gives birth to his little sister, in the second his dog's run over and in the third his fiancée is, "Too good for this earth and taken by the angels." His voice cracked with emotion at poignant parts of the song.

He walked off the stage to chanting from the crowd of, "We love you Triple B!" That's how his fans, and there were so many of them, addressed their iconic musical hero. His full name was Billy-Bob Bingham the Third. His broad grin went off as if God had thrown a switch. A roadie handed him a monogrammed towel to wipe his face. Billy-Bob threw it down, shouting, "Wrong frickin' colour." Another back stage crew member handed him a blue towel. This seemed to appease Billy-Bob slightly and he strode in the direction of his dressing room, mopping the sweat from his face, glowering at anyone who dared look at him.

His agent was waiting in his dressing room for him. She stood with a calculator in her hand.

"You sure killed 'em tonight. T-shirt sales are up 12 percent and the merchandise is flyin' off the shelves. They can't get enough of you, Triple B," she said with a huge grin on her heavily made-up face.

Billy-Bob simply grunted as he took off his plaid shirt, not bothering to undo the buttons. There was always somebody on the payroll for those menial tasks. He sat down and faced the mirror and spoke to her without turning around.

"Call that a big theatre? I've seen bigger hog pens."

She moved up to him and rubbed his shoulders and talked to him in the mirror.

"Now, Billy-Bob, you're not bein' fair to old Angie. It's in my best interest to book you into the largest venues and this is the biggest that this city has."

"Well, I'm tired of playin' these one horse towns. When am I gonna be playin' the Grand ol' Opry?"

"Patience, Triple B. You stick with me, boy and I'll make you the biggest country-and-western star the world's ever seen. That kinda success don't come over night. You and me are playin' the long game. Remember when I first heard you sing in that honkytonk bar in Nashville? Singin' along to a karaoke machine? Well I saw then what all your fans are seeing now. I reckon we'll be lookin' at you bein' enrolled in the country music hall of fame within the next few years."

This put a smile on Billy-Bob's face for the first time since he'd come off stage.

"D'ya reckon?"

She nodded then gave him a stack of head shots of himself to sign. "Autograph these and I'll distribute them to the stage door groupies. Are you in the mood for some of them comin' back to the dressin' room?"

"Hell no! I want me some peace and quiet."

"Well in that case, I'll leave you to it." She picked up the photographs that he'd scribbled hastily across and left his dressing room.

Just 30 seconds after Angie had left, there was a knock at the door.

He wished he'd brought a 'Do not Disturb' sign with him from the hotel. He yelled, "I'm busy." Whoever it was, either hadn't heard or wouldn't take the hint.

There was another knock, this time more insistent and louder. He got out of his chair and went to the door and opened it.

"Are you deaf or somethin'?"

The woman in front of him simply smiled. She was a woman in her 60s, dressed very smartly. Then after a few seconds she spoke in a South London accent, "It must be exhausting for you, dear."

Billy-Bob had a puzzled expression. "Sorry, ma'am, about hollerin' like that, but can I help you?"

When she didn't answer he continued, "Would you like an autograph? Would you like me to sign one of my posters or CDs?"

She smiled again and shook her head. "I've got enough of those back home, Lance, or rather Julie has. All those letters you wrote her. Surely you remember?"

He hadn't heard those two names in a long while. He rubbed his eyes and took another look at the person in front of him. This wasn't a sad, lonely middle aged woman in awe of her idol. She did seem familiar.

"What did you mean about it being exhausting? D'ya mean the touring life? Well, it can get to you when you haven't slept in your own–"

"I think I'd better come in, dear."

She walked into his dressing room and closed the door behind her. She didn't wait to be offered a chair before she sat down. Billy-Bob followed and pulled a chair across to face her.

"Shall we stop all this nonsense, dear? You've got no audience to impress now we're behind closed doors. You can stop that silly accent now as well, it's getting on my nerves. I'm surprised these Americans fall for it. They must be really gullible."

Billy-Bob helped himself to a swig of whisky and then

handed her the bottle.

She waved it away. "No thank you, dear. I'm surprised you indulge after what it did to your poor mother. Your dad kept finding bottles all over the place. I think that's what started you off on the binge eating. Morbidly obese, wasn't it Lance?"

"My name is Billy-Bob, ma'am," he said in an unconvincing transatlantic drawl.

"We both know that's not true, Lance. Let's not pretend."

After a short while he spoke. "It was clinically obese, actually." This was the first time that he'd spoken in his native London voice for years.

"That's better, Lance. Now I can understand you properly." She leant across and patted him on the knee.

"It's lovely to see you again after all these years. I don't understand how you managed to lose so much weight and make yourself so much taller."

"The lifts in my boots give me an extra three inches and the heels are pretty high. A gastric band sorted out the weight loss."

He seemed relieved to be able to be honest to somebody. "How did you recognise me, Mrs Sinclair?"

"I was there when your mum and dad brought you home from the hospital. I was pregnant with Julie at the time. Your mum and I joked that you two would end up getting married. You spent as much time in our house as you did your own when you were at primary school together. Thick as thieves the pair of you. Then you seemed to drift apart as teenagers. Then you started piling on the pounds and then the valentines started. We knew they were from you. I recognised the handwriting. I told Julie to let you down gently. We didn't see much of you when you went away to college, then your parents split up and sold the house. How long ago was that?"

"19 years."

She had a broad grin on her face. She stood up and hugged him. "Now look at you! The big success. But why did you have to choose that stupid name and why on earth pretend to be a Yank?"

It was Lance's turn to smile. "How many country-and-western stars do you know who come from Croydon? And my real name hardly did me any favours."

She explained she was on an organised tour and that she'd discovered by chance that he was playing that night.

"I recognised you straight away from the posters outside. Couldn't believe my luck. I think I got the last ticket. You do seem ever so popular. Your parents would have been ever so proud of you."

Angie walked into the room and Lance introduced her to Mrs Sinclair. Although Angie smiled at the other woman, the facial expression lacked any warmth.

"Do you mind leaving us alone for a minute please, Triple B?" Although it was a question, Angie clearly expected him to leave.

He stepped out of the room and walked up and down the corridor. He returned a few minutes later.

Mrs Sinclair was lying lifeless on the floor.

Angie didn't let him speak. She made sure the door was closed. "I had to protect my investment. Word gets out that you're a Brit and we're dead in the water. D'ya wanna know how much money I've poured into your image?"

Lance had never seen his manager look so menacing before.

"But there was no need to kill her."

"Oh yes there was, hon. I know her type. Turning up like this in your dressing room was no coincidence. This just proves that you need me as your manager steering you to the big time. On your own, you'd probably fall for every sob story going. I found this in her handbag.

She handed him an envelope addressed to him. Inside was a letter in Mrs Sinclair's handwriting giving details of her bank account, explaining that the cost of her silence was a cool 1m pounds.

~

Andrew Campbell-Kearsey's Biography

I was a primary head teacher in another life. Now I make things up. I've had two collections of short stories published and a couple of short films made of my work. Thorny Devil Productions are currently pitching a television series based on my short stories.

My second film, *A Quiet Courage* based on my short story 'A Dangerous Precedent' was screened at the Tenth Hollyshorts Film Festival in Los Angeles in August 2014, starring Louise Jameson and Annette Badland.

THE EXTRAORDINARY DIARY OF A 23RD CENTURY TEENAGER

Shortlisted story, by JR Hampton

Saturday, 1st July 2215

Dear Sam,

I think I'm in love. The universe is a wonderful place. This afternoon a new family moved into the old Mainwaring's house across the road. Oh Sam, she was amazing. I tinted the windows so that she couldn't see me. I think she's an Altarian girl. Altarians are so good-looking. She has the most perfect green skin, beautiful deep blue eyes and the cutest dimples in the galaxy! I think this time she could really be the one. I think she might be clever too because she was carrying an electronic book reader and her parents drive a Ford skycar.

I watched her all day moving from window to window, her pretty head bobbing to and fro like a little electronic bee.

She likes the Beta Boys. I know this because I saw her carrying in a big e-poster of them. I don't like boy-bands. I'll have to introduce her to some Rigelian jazz.

I think if we get married, I am going to move to Mars. She would like it there. She will probably be a writer, or maybe a journalist. I'll be a space pilot. We'll have two children and a holographic dog. When she gets older, she'll want to have genetic surgery, but I won't let her because I'll tell her that she's beautiful without it.

Oh Sam. What shall I do? How can I make her know that I am here, two star crossed lovers parted only by an insignificant road on an insignificant planet?

Sunday, 2nd July 2215

Dear Sam,

It's official. Brian Ponsonby is my nemesis! I hate his guts. Just because he has a bionic arm it doesn't make him special. I mean, what can she see in *him*? Next time he comes to me asking for someone to go hover-boarding with, I am going to… well I am just not going to go, he'll have to find someone else. He knows that I like Altarian girls too.

This morning when I woke up, all I could think about was *her*. And right from the off she was really beginning to irritate me. I had to wait 'til almost 10am until she bothered to show and then that was only at the downstairs window for about one millisecond.

Then, to make matters worse, when I came back from the toilet I'd noticed that their skycar was gone! Can you imagine, I am sat there for hours with the windows tinted, still in my pyjamas and she didn't have the decency to come outside even once!

And then I also had to contend with Mum. All day she kept going on and on about how I was a gloomy teenager and that I shouldn't be sat in the dark all day. She doesn't know about love, not about true love, that's why she's married to Dad.

Anyway, the reason I am so angry tonight is because after dinner I saw Brian and his family going over to her house. They were stood in the porch for ages! He was all like, I'm Brian, look at my arm and she was all like, ooh a bionic arm! And then he was showing off on his hover-board, but what she doesn't know yet, is that I taught Brian everything he knows. When she finally meets me, she'll feel a bit of an idiot for even talking to him.

Eventually, Brian's mum finally shut up so she was able to get away from him.

I am just going to try and relax tonight now. It's been a stressful day. I think I might listen to some Rigelian jazz to calm me down.

Monday, 3rd July 2215

Dear Sam,

Well, well, well. Another day wasted waiting for 'Princess of the Universe' to grace me with her presence. And to top it off, I was staring at the front upstairs window for about half an hour today, absorbed in the silhouette of her graceful head until I realised that it was the reflection from a street lamp. Maybe she'll honour me with her presence tomorrow before I waste my entire summer holiday on her.

Wednesday, 5th July 2215

Dear Sam,

I have noticed that the Cholmondeley's at number 11 have a 4D Virtual Reality TV. How can they afford one of them? I know for a fact that Mr Cholmondeley has been out of work since he got fired from the Robot Repair Shop and Mrs Cholmondeley only earns a pittance at Admiral Atom's Cloneburger Restaurant. Life's just not fair. On the upside, I have now completed all of the Professor Pixel games on my Megabox. No sign of the Princess again.

I have another theory. I was reading on the instellarnet about how people in the olden days used to mistake space-time mirages for ghosts of dead people. The man who made the discovery, Dr Stephen Cowper, explained that it was such an improbable event that led his younger self to encounter his own 94 year old space-time mirage, then inform him of the anomaly, that all sorts of other things in the cosmos could be going on all around us and we would just not have the faintest idea that they were happening. Well, I think it's the same with me and the Princess. I am going on across the road from her, and she doesn't have a clue that I am here.

Friday, 7th July 2215

Dear Sam,

I think something is going on between Mr Wodehouse and Miss Beaulieu. I saw him go into her house at 11am this morning and he didn't leave until gone 4pm. I am thinking about leaving a note for Mrs Wodehouse to let her know what's going on. Also, I noticed that one of the solar tiles on our new neighbour's roof is loose. I may tell Mrs Ponsonby so that she can inform them.

Saturday, 8th July 2215

Dear Sam,

What is Princess Perfect's problem? Is she some sort of demented hermit? I had to avoid Brian three times today, blarting on about going hover-boarding as usual. I told Mum I thought I was coming down with a bout of Polluxian Pox so he'd leave me alone. Also, I only just realised today that the Princess has a younger brother! He was freaking me out because he sat at the downstairs window for about 20 minutes staring at my window. He couldn't have seen me because I definitely checked that my window was tinted. He looks a little bit like the Princess. I hope I haven't been getting them mixed up.

Tuesday, 11th July 2215

Dear Sam,

I think I caught the back of the Princess's head today when she was leaving in the skycar, although I can't be sure now I know that she has a brother with the same type of spherical head. I am sure there is something going on between Mr Wodehouse and Miss Beaulieu, he was around her house again today, from 9.30am to

5pm, then, later, in the evening, I saw Mr and Mrs Wodehouse having an argument in their front room and then she stormed off upstairs and sat crying in the front bedroom for ages. The solar panel seems to have fallen about quarter of a centimetre since Friday. I've started to get into *Dr Belvoir Investigates*. It's about a doctor who solves murders in Old New York City. I didn't realise it was so good.

I think I will be a doctor when I am older, or maybe a detective.

Thursday, 13th July 2215

Dear Sam,

I have a theory. First, why does the Princess stay inside her house so much? Well, to answer this I deduce that because she is Altarian, she must have a different resistance to our solar rays. She will have to acclimatise to our environment before she can risk going outdoors. It makes perfect sense. I also deduce that she may be emotionally vulnerable due to the move from such an advanced star system to our pitiful planet. This would result in a mild form of depression, whereby she would seek asylum in the depths of one of her books, probably a soppy romance about some cosmic knight rescuing a Denebian damsel from the clutches of a Vegan triple headed dwarf. It would probably be a saga and therefore take her a long time to read. Girls like that type of stuff.

To investigate my theory, I have created a techno sensorscope on my 4D printer. I have aligned it to the opposite bedroom window to detect any e-readers and download the content to my data-card. If I can figure out what she is reading, I may be able to use it as the theme for our first date.

I have been researching Altair on the interstellarnet. Apparently the Altarian alphabet contains over 1,000 characters, they are the largest exporter of cheese in the universe, it is home to the universe's smallest tree, the Altarian parrot has a vocabulary of over 1m words, they consume more cosmic latte than any other planet, 89% of the population are left handed and it is the birthplace of Zalfreid Dunderpop, inventor of the first laser guided toothbrush.

Friday, 14th July 2215

Dear Sam,

I am in trouble. Princess's father complained that his anti-theft alarm system had picked up a signal from our house last night, waking him up in the early hours. It took over two hours for my dad to calm him down. I erased the sensorscope and denied everything. Luckily the police decided only to give my dad a caution. Dad wanted to ground me, but my mum insisted that he didn't and that he should take me out of the house. Guess who's going to the museum tomorrow!

Did you know? Altarians eat over 3m tons of hydrated potato a year!

Saturday, 15th July 2215

Dear Sam,

The museum was awesome! I bought a new sonic pen to write in you with. It has a picture of an old fashioned aeroplane on it.

I got to see some mega stuff in there. They have the largest collection of carrier bags on the planet. Did you know that humans in the 21st century used to be three inches shorter on average, many people on the planet did not have enough food and water and died as a result, they did not have access to the interstellarnet and had to rely on only a planetary internet, only men were permitted to wear moustaches, processed sugar based foods were popular with children, in hospitals, surgeons would actually cut open your body to fix you and they produced so much pollution that they almost destroyed the planet.

They had a special exhibition on Dr Cornelius Taliaferro, the actual inventor of time travel. Did you know that he invented a time machine 25 years after inventing time travel because the first time he explored history his machine broke down so he had to re-invent it to get back home? By the time he arrived back in his own time period, time travel was a bit old hat and the planetary government had made it illegal. He was promptly arrested and was released next Thursday.

When we got back, I saw Mr Wodehouse arguing with Miss Beaulieu. She looked really upset. I bet he has decided to stop seeing her. Also, I noticed the Princess's dad has installed tinted windows in their house. I wonder if he is an overprotective father and is keeping her caged in like a Capellanese double crested tetrapod. Apparently, Brian Ponsonby tried calling for me five times when I was at the museum! Talk about needy!

Wednesday, 19th July 2215

Dear Sam,

I saw the Princess today! I was at my window on watch for any movement from the new neighbour's front door when a galactic taxi arrived. An old Altarian lady came out in a hover-chair and glided up to the porch. Next thing, I could see the Princess's mother dallying around. I almost missed my glimpse of the Princess because the stupid old lady's chair kept hovering up in the way.

Eventually the old bat flew in and for the briefest of nanoseconds, I swear our eyes met. She must have sensed that there was something fundamental to her life, lurking behind the veiled panes of glass. As quickly as she appeared, she had gone. The universe can be cruel like that.

Did you know? The Tarazedans, who are from the same constellation as Altair, cannot walk backwards.

Friday, 21st July 2215

Dear Sam,

No sign of the Princess today, again. I feel like I am going insane! I haven't cleaned my teeth for three days now because my laser toothbrush is broken. I keep meaning to tell Mum to get me a new one but I am just so busy, I haven't had the time.

Dr Belvoir Investigates was brilliant today. It had an awesome twist at the end where the murder was in fact suicide by time travel. Dr Belvoir is so clever.

Thursday, 27th July 2215

Dear Sam,

I was watching a Startube documentary today. It was all about a man from Alpha Centuri who fell into a black hole. Apparently, he emerged from a white hole and met a photo-negative version of himself. It was definitely true because on the video he showed some photo's he'd taken of himself on his mobile device, but they had all reverted to the opposite colours when he travelled back through the white hole.

I have a theory. I reckon that there could be an infinite number of Princesses and I who are all in love in countless multi-dimensions and that's why we are destined to meet in this one.

I am thinking of becoming a scientist when I am older.

Did you know? The Altarian spinning top was originally used as a weapon by their ancestors.

Sunday, 30th July 2215

Dear Sam,

I watched Brian Ponsonby showing off outside the Princess's house today on his hover-board. If he thinks he can impress her with his inferior skills, well he is very much mistaken. I am so proud of her; she didn't rise to the bait once.

Did you know? There is no equivalent word for sausage in the Altarian language.

Monday, 7th August 2215

Dear Sam,

I think I am in trouble again. Miss Beaulieu was at our house today crying. Mum says that she has fallen out with Mrs Wodehouse because she was secretly helping Mr Wodehouse plan a silver wedding anniversary surprise. Apparently, Mrs Wodehouse doesn't believe her because she received an anonymous note from one of the neighbours informing her of their affair. Mum says that the Wodehouse's may even end up getting a divorce. That's what you get for keeping secrets.

Friday, 11th August 2215

Dear Sam,

I finally know her name, it's Zara! Apparently Brian has been trying to get me to go hover-boarding with her for over a month because he knows that I like Altarians and she thinks I'm lonely and a bit odd because Altarians can see through tinted windows, apparently. Strange that it doesn't mention this on the interstellarnet.

Oh I am so happy! This morning Brian finally got around to calling for me when I was in, and he told me all about her.

Her family have moved to Earth because her father is a climate control engineer and we are one of the last planets where he can find work. Her mum is a surgeon and has landed a top job at the local hospital. And guess what? You'll never believe this! Zara and her brother are going to be going to the same school as me, Richard Dawkin's Comprehensive, and her parents have asked if Brian and I will take care of her and help her to fit in. That means I am going to get to see her every day!

Brian says that they have been hanging around at Attenborough Park every day but he usually meets her there, because her family have a transporter booth. I have been right about Zara too. Brian says she is really clever and she has been asking loads of questions about me.

I don't think I'm going to sleep tonight; I'm too excited about tomorrow. We are meeting her at the park at 10am. I'm going to put on some Rigelian jazz to calm my nerves.

Did you know? An Altarian's heart beats faster than a human's.

Saturday, 12th August 2215

Dear Sam,

Well, what a disappointment Zara turned out to be. We met at the park as planned and I started by showing off some of my skills on the hover-board. I think she missed all of my best stunts because she had her big abnormal head stuck in her e-reader all the time. Then when I was trying to make polite conversation by talking about *Dr Belvoir Investigates*, because her mum is a doctor, she told me not to sit so close because my breath stank and that in the Altarian culture, dental hygiene is considered paramount. Then, she went on to criticize *Dr Belvoir* because she thinks it's a formulaic show for childish minds as the doctor always solves the case at the end by resuscitating the victim. If she was so smart, she'd realise that that is the whole reason why it works so well because if he resuscitated the victims at the beginning, then there'd be no story. Duh!

Brian was no better either. Every time she uttered something out of her nonexistent lips, he agreed with her instead of me! And he's supposed to be *my* best friend!

Anyway, it was not all bad. When I got home, I saw Zara's dad having a tantrum because one of the solar tiles had fallen from their roof and Brian's parents were taking the brunt of it because they said they'd known about it for ages but forgot to say. Serves them all right!

Monday, 14th August 2215

Dear Sam,

I'm dreading the start of school. I am going to be stuck with Brian and Zara following me about for a whole year.

Did you know? 13% of Altarians still believe in the Big Bang. Idiots.

~

Julian Hampton's Biography

Mr JR Hampton resides in a quaint little house on a quaint little cul-de-sac in a quaint little city named Coventry. He teaches English and Maths at a quaint little college. How did he come to be?

Well, let's suppose that some time in history, Douglas Adams and Sue Townsend collided at an incredible speed at CERN's Large Hadron Collider in Switzerland. One night, when a technician was cleaning up the mess he discovered lying in the tunnel, a half written story titled 'The Extraordinary Diary of a 23rd Century Teenager' by JR Hampton. Well, the universe had to do something about this right away so, out of thin air, up popped JR Hampton on a sofa, in a quaint little house in Coventry, who instantly declared an idea for a story he'd just had.

THE HAUNTING OF ADRIAN DELACROIX

Shortlisted story, by Ben Langley

The séance was a last resort.

Adrian Delacroix had put up with it for six months. It started with missing keys. Every evening when he got in from work, usually late after agreeing to do half a dozen 'just one more things', he hung his keys on the hook on the back of the door. In the morning they'd be gone, but after searching for half an hour he would find them, on the door where he'd left them.

The optician told him his eyes were fine.

Then the keys stopped reappearing on the hook and would turn up in the fridge, the microwave or behind the toilet in that hard to reach spot where the spiders always loitered.

Adrian was worried that if he was moving them, but unaware of his actions, he might have a serious problem but after visiting the doctors and being referred to a psychiatrist he was given a clean bill of mental health.

Things only got stranger after that. He'd wake to find his living room furniture rearranged, his DVD collection un-alphabetised, or all of his shirt sleeves tied together.

He called his sister for help. Michelle was a big fan of the *Paranormal Activity* movies, and had access to a lot of recording equipment. She was waiting outside his apartment when he arrived home from work, arms laden with files.

"Are you bringing work home again?" said Michelle as she stood. She was wearing those enormous hoop earrings that Adrian had never dared tell her that he hated.

"Hi Sis, nice to see you."

"Do you even get paid for all this extra work you do?" said Michelle.

"No, but–"

"No but nothing. Just say 'No' Adrian. Don't be such a bloody pushover."

"I'm trying to get caught up, hunting for my keys for an hour each morning means I'm always late."

"Well I've got the cameras," said Michelle, gesturing to the box she'd been sitting on. "So hopefully we'll get to the bottom of this."

But all the cameras managed to prove was that Adrian spent the whole night in bed, so he wasn't the one who'd been into the kitchen and turned the table over.

"You caught nothing on the camera?"

"No it blipped for a second, then it was done."

"What can it be then?"

"I guess it's some kind of poltergeist," said Michelle as Adrian flipped the table back.

"I'd offer you a tea, but the kettle's gone," said Adrian.

"I know you don't believe in this kind of stuff, but I know this spirit medium. She might be able to help."

"I don't know what else to do," said Adrian. "I guess it's worth a shot."

Michelle pulled out her phone and left the room. When she came back Adrian was sniffing the herbs.

"The labels have been switched! I don't know which is basil and which is Herbs de Provence!"

"Mistress Goulbourne can come on Thursday," said Michelle.

*

Michelle stayed until Thursday and kept the cameras rolling, but every night they'd go fuzzy before anything weird happened. Wednesday morning they woke up to find water all over the kitchen floor as a result of the freezer having defrosted after being switched off. On Thursday Adrian had to pick up spare underwear on the way to work as every single pair had been shrunk to half its size.

On Thursday evening, Michelle was packing her cameras away.

"So we can't record it then?"

"No, that's one of her conditions."

"And you're sure she's not some charlatan?"

There was a knock on the door.

"She probably heard that," said Michelle.

Mistress Goulbourne was a waddler, had hair like a 1980s American wrestler, and spoke entirely in clichés.

"I can feel a presence in the room," she said before she'd even taken her coat off.

Adrian sat at his round dinner table, pulled out into the centre of the kitchen, with Michelle on his left and Mistress Goulbourne on the right. He couldn't keep his eyes off the ketchup stain on the table and cringed every time Mistress Goulbourne's long sleeves swept over it. This séance was costing enough, he didn't want to fork out for her dry cleaning too.

"He who haunts this gentleman – walk into the light."

The lights flickered. Michelle squeezed Adrian's hand, but Mistress Goulbourne rolled her eyes, "Not that light. Our spiritual light."

The outline of a man started to form, floating above the table.

"Why do you remain on this astral plain when you could find peace on the other side?"

"Revenge," said the ghostly shape.

"What for?" said Adrian squinting at the translucent figure.

"You know what you did," said the ghost.

"Who is it?" asked Michelle.

"I don't know," said Adrian.

"You don't remember?" said the ghost. "You tormented me!"

The kitchen roll unravelled itself onto the floor.

"Think back," said Mistress Goulbourne, "what did you do to this poor soul that he might bare a grudge that lasts beyond his lifetime?"

"I can't think of anyone. Who are you?"

"My name... is Wayne Plumb."

"I don't know a Wayne Plumb."

"Maybe you remember me better as Dumb Plumb... That's what you called me."

"No..."

"You and your friends tormented me. Itching power down my back. Poison ivy hidden in my PE Kit."

"I didn't."

"You made my life at St. Peter's hell!"

The utensils drawer floated out and cutlery jumped overboard and clattered onto the floor.

"I... never went to St Peter's. I don't even know where that is..." said Adrian.

"Lies!"

"It's true," said Michelle, "we both went to Thamesview."

"Wait..." said Wayne. "You are Alan Delacroix?"

"No."

"Born 18th March 1968?"

"No! My name's Adrian, born June 79!"

"Oh," said Wayne.

"So you've made my life a bloody nightmare for no good reason?"

"Well it's not a common name, I didn't think I'd find another Delacroix."

"Do I even look the same? I'm over 10 years younger for one thing."

"Well, it was such a long time ago. What can I do to make it up to you?"

"You could start by sorting this place out."

The spirit wound the kitchen roll back up and picked up the knives and forks.

"And where's my bloody kettle?" said Adrian.

"Airing cupboard. Wrapped in the big beige towel."

Wayne started to shimmer. His image thinned.

"Come back here," said Adrian.

"What more can I do? I made a mistake. Can't we all move on?"

"You can apologise."

"Yes. I guess I should," said Wayne. He bowed, and before he disappeared from Adrian's life forever he said, "Frightfully sorry."

~

Ben Langley's Biography

Benjamin J Langley graduated from Anglia Ruskin University in 2012 where he was awarded the Katy Price Prize for the best major writing project. He is currently studying towards an MA in Creative Writing and is working on his first novel. His fiction has been published by *Dark Tales*, *Words with Jam*, and *Skive Magazine* and he has had comedy sketches broadcast on ITV and on BBC digital radio.

THE KEYCOCK

Shortlisted story, by Keith Newton

Like many of my friends I leapt eagerly into retirement, determined to enjoy, at last, the many activities supposedly precluded by a busy working life. Meticulously, we crossed off the items on our lists: the ancient ruins and historic piles we had somehow missed, the museums and galleries unvisited, books unread, golf courses unplayed. We agreed with each other that the great thing about the grueling new regimen was that it was self-imposed. We confided privately that it was tiring. Some said tiresome. We stuck doggedly to the basics, of course: exercise, sensible diet (most of the time), cryptic crosswords, and all that. We took up the unfinished projects... and set them aside again. Then some started to get the urge. To write, I mean.

Conversations slowly shifted away from someone's hole-in-one, the latest dirt on a politician or rock star, or Archie's new hip. Allusions to allegory, archetype and voice crept in. Assonance, I learned, did not mean being stupid. Soon it was 'character development' (not, apparently, Girl Guides or speleology). Narrative arcs, complete with apotheoses, were introduced with increasing confidence. At first I found it a bit pretentious. Gradually, grudgingly, I began to find it fascinating. So when I was asked, quite seriously, what was my particular *genre,* I quickly retrieved that new-found word and modestly mouthed the first thing that entered my head: travel. The word was out. ("Heard you're doing a bit of writing too. Travel, eh? Good show. Can't wait to see your stuff.") *Gawd.* I was stuck. Travel writer. *Wannabe. Maybe.*

I plunged into research, immersing myself in travel stories, reading voraciously until I felt ready to draw some tentative conclusions. Travel stories, I decided, are often about terribly interesting, exotic, exciting, exquisitely beautiful places; or at least quaint, charming, or characterful ones. Less often the places described are bleak, ugly, god-forsaken. The stories may involve characters good or evil, happy or sad, inspiring or depressing. There may be an adventure, emotional or physical. It might be hair-raising but fun; life-threatening or marvelously transporting.

My story does not obviously contain such proven ingredients. Its particular location doesn't matter; it could have happened almost anywhere. It's not about societies-cultures-museums-cuisines; no soaring spires or weathered gargoyles. No frangipani-scented warm evening air, moon-shimmered lake 'neath the dark, diamond–studded velvety celestial vault. No tinkling temple bells in the distance as almond eyes glisten below blue-black raven hair. No grizzled walnut visages creased in gap-toothed tobacco-stained grins... not forgetting the mud-crusted sabots or ice-stiff mukluks, of course. And this little tale contains no vividly-drawn characters; just the teeniest of cameos by a concierge and a plumber and his lad.

The setting for my adventure was a small hotel in the seventeenth century market square within a large Belgian city. Trailing my suitcase over the bumpy cobblestones I took in the inevitable fountain, the benches and the statues of civic worthies and a couple of saints. Narrow streets radiated spoke-like from the square. The various cafes and bistros suggested a promising evening of selecting vantage points from which to enjoy the passing parade, checking out menus, and sampling the local fare. The hotel itself met my expectations nicely. It was tall and thin with a protruding beam and its iron ring high up on the facade. I imagined the block and tackle, the rope, the pulley and the great hook as, long ago, the local carters, muscles bulging, loaded or unloaded merchandise. Or, better still, the same stalwarts holding fast as a sturdy four-poster dangled outside a fifth-floor window.

I entered happily. The desk clerk reluctantly tore himself away from the soccer game on TV and to my relief confirmed my reservation and handed me the key. Ah, the key. It was attached to a very heavy thick iron rod with a bulge at the end and a number stamped on it: 152.

"Cent cinquante-deux," I confirmed.

"Yes," he told me, "fifth floor."

"But," I ventured hesitantly, "it says one 52."

"It has a five in it," I was told, "they all do on the fifth floor." With this he turned back to the game.

I stood for a moment, pondering the logic of that last response, hefting the weighty lump in my hand. A glance at the pigeon-holes behind the clerk's counter suggested a reason for the cudgel's existence. You evidently had to leave your key behind whenever you went out. The weight would certainly help you to remember; you sure wouldn't want to tour the Grand Place with that in your pocket. But what was it exactly? Did it have a name? My vocabulary failed me. It did look rather like... good heavens... yes, that was it! A keycock!

Pleased with this verbal innovation I hoisted my shoulder-bag and trundled my suitcase to the elevator, where a push on the button produced a grating sound, then light behind the semi-opaque glass door. I entered. The light went out. I felt for the buttons, guessed there was one basement level and that the main floor would be zero (it had been in Paris) and counted up to five. Pressed. The light came on. The cramped cubicle started upwards. I soon noticed that it had only two sides, and watched the dark walls of the elevator shaft gliding by, with occasional flashes of light as we passed the four floors on the way up to mine. At floor five the door responded to my shove and revealed a short, narrow corridor not much wider than the elevator itself. Ahead of me through the gloom I made out three doors with numbers, one of which was mine. Another door bore a strange sign which I judged to indicate exit stairs. *So far so good. Now try the key.*

It went in all right, with just a modicum of jiggling. It turned nicely and gave a satisfying click. I shoved. No luck. I cajoled the door handle. Shoved harder. Jollied the key a bit, keycock banging on the door. Felt I might give it one more turn. Tough. Sweat. *Bloody keycock.* Another click: *Yes!* I was in. But so was the key: stuck in the lock, and it wouldn't come out. *Damn it. Leave it. Get in.*

The short, narrow hallway of the room might have been wide enough for me and my trailing suitcase had it not been for the inexplicable presence of a long narrow table jammed up against the left wall. I stood the case, pushed in its drag-handle and nudged it down the little hall with my knee. Before edging carefully past the mysterious table, I noted on my left a door-less alcove. Glancing in I noted approvingly a gleaming basin, mirror and faucets, and a plastic curtain which I judged to conceal a shower. A few more nudges brought me and the suitcase to the sleeping area. A bed on my left was jammed to the wall, its head to what must have been the back of the shower-stall and its foot at the outer wall of the hotel. I dropped my tote bag on the bed and stood with my suitcase, more or less filling the space between the bed and two exceedingly narrow ceiling-high cupboards. The cupboards weren't deep. I opened one to find a rod on which a few metal hangers were angled so as to fit. No room for the suitcase. It would just have to lie on the floor. I sat on the bed. It was hard but I cared only that the sheets were clean and crisp. *Oh well.* I eased gratefully out of my sneakers. At that moment I just wanted to have a shower then go out to the nearest café, bar, whatever, for a cold one with the newspaper and the passing parade. But I'd left the door open with the key still in it.

The keycock hung sullenly, daring me to rejoin the battle. I did. With the door still open I was able to turn the key back to the locked position. *OK, so at least I know that locking this beauty should be a breeze. Now, turn it back to the open position.* Two satisfying clicks and the deadbolt withdrew. *Good. Close door. Pull out key.* But the key held fast. I tugged. The keycock leered. I sweated. Grabbing the wretched thing with both hands I pulled harder. The thick steel wire connecting the key to the bludgeon yielded to the force. Fortunately the little hallway was so narrow that the distance between my head and the wall was short. I bumped and slumped to my backside, still clutching the keycock. The key was still in the door. Expletive. *Be calm. Take it easy. Shower.* Disgruntled, I held the rod in one hand and made to reenter; paused; gave the key a little jiggle; pulled half-heartedly. Out it came, smooth as you like. Expletives. Shower.

It was a familiar design. Two taps to adjust for water temperature and a shower head at the end of a long, snake-like flexible tube. The shower head could be hand-held to reach out-of-the-way body parts or held at the desired height by a clip on a vertical rod. The snake lay motionless on the floor of the shower stall. I turned on the taps and tested for the required temperature, then adjusted further for more force. The sudden surge blew the shower head off. The snake leapt and writhed and squirmed spasmodically, lashing angrily. I stumbled naked, half in and half out of the shower as fierce spurts of water drenched me, the tiny 'bathroom' and, alas, the towels. I wrestled the taps closed, splodged two steps to the passageway and edged past the mysterious table to the bed.

I extricated a more-or-less clean T-shirt from my case and dried off. What to do? If I were to tell the clerk I had a problem with the shower he might treat it as the routine complaint of yet another picky foreigner. But, although the requisite repair was quite simple – requiring just enough brute force to re-attach the shower head firmly to the connector on the hose – I wasn't sure that my albeit-reasonable French was up to the task of explaining this plumbing job. So I quickly pulled out pen and paper and sketched the two articles that should be reunited. Dressed, I collected the keycock, and the (now separate) key, along with my diagram and prepared to descend. Breathing deeply and with a silent prayer I successfully locked the door behind me and with very little persuasion extracted the key. It, and the lock and I, were clearly getting along much better.

Two things occurred to me as I turned towards the elevator. First, now would be a good time to pee before going to a bistro where, for sure, I would be faced with a narrow, dark, steep serpentine climb or descent. Second, there was no toilet in my room and the other doors in the gloomy little hallway led to rooms or the stairway. I decided to take up this matter at the desk. Clutching my items for the show-and-tell I entered the lift and, unfazed by the light's caprice, stood carefully in its centre. I confidently selected the correct button.

I was mightily relieved that the clerk did not erupt when I showed him the broken steel connecting wire. In fact he seemed very amused and, I thought, rather impressed. He rummaged for some time beneath his counter and emerged triumphantly with enormous pliers with which, with considerable strength, he reshaped the steel connector to join the keycock and key once again. "Voila", he grinned, and popped them into their pigeon hole. I then proffered the diagram, which he took very seriously, stroking his moustache and fixing me with a keen gaze. Reaching for the phone he assured me that his friend the plumber would arrive in no time. So far, so good. Timorously, I enquired about the toilet. Yes, he confirmed patiently, it was just outside my door, on the landing. Top floor. How could I have missed it? Chastened, I rode the lift again and stood baffled in the gloomy little hallway. I checked the doors with the numbers and pushed open the remaining door which, sure enough, led onto a staircase. I turned and faced the elevator and there, barely visible in the dark corner, the carpet branched off to reveal, on closer inspection, four steps leading upwards. *Ha!* So mine wasn't the top floor. I stumbled up the steps, feeling the walls for a light switch. Contact! Light appeared around the cracks of a door frame. Success. Or so I thought until I closed the door behind me and the light went out. I stroked the walls and found no switch, but the light came on again. Of course; it was motion-sensitive. I soon found that a gentle rocking motion – such as some might adopt during the study of certain religious texts – seemed sufficient to keep the light on.

The descent to the lobby was uneventful – I was an old hand by now – and I sailed out to find, just a few steps away, a sunny table where I ordered a much-needed drink. On the patio were a few locals and a few obvious tourists including a gaggle of Orientals brandishing cameras enthusiastically. I enjoyed the atmosphere and the refreshment, glancing over my newspaper occasionally to observe the passers-by. A 'character' appeared. Burly, florid, grizzled, wearing a crumpled wool cap, a faded blue work shirt, weathered waistcoat, corduroy trousers and stout boots. He seated himself so as to look directly through the window of the hotel's little breakfast room. He looked quickly at his watch, produced a newspaper and a pipe and ordered a large flask of red wine.

I finished my drink, paid, and reentered the hotel. The plumbing job – he made it sound like a major construction project – had been completed, the desk clerk told me. However, I could not go to my room as the cleaning lady had yet to go and mop up "le deluge."

"Fine," I said, "may I use the internet?"

One euro secured a half-hour connection and in a corner of the little breakfast room I caught up with some of the folks back home.

As I logged off I became aware of a presence beside me. I looked down to see long pointed shoes. Then, as my gaze moved upwards, impossibly tight jeans, a tattooed forearm, singlet, and atop all this some scraggly whiskers attached to an absurdly youthful grinning face.

"M'mselle," it told me, "your phone, it is fixed."

Now, I certainly knew enough French to recognize the word 'telephone' but didn't catch on immediately. There was no phone in my room. Then, of course, I realised that the shower head is shaped very much like one half of the receiver of a standard telephone. A cupped hand appeared and the grin broadened when I dropped a few euros into it. Looking up I saw through the window the crumpled hat and, between it and the top edge of his newspaper, the beaming face of the gentleman on the patio. Master and apprentice, I surmised. The three of us enjoyed a drink together. Hearty wine, sunshine and a job well done.

~

Keith Newton's Biography

Keith was born and educated in the North East of England, went to Canada to pursue further studies and stayed there to teach. As a researcher and professor of Economics 'publish or perish' was part of the game so he has put out several dozen articles and books. He has taught at several universities, headed numerous research teams, advised governments and lectured in a dozen countries. A year in Australia was professionally productive and culturally stimulating: good work-mates, opera, cricket and beer.

An ageing athlete, he enjoys most of the fine arts (in which he includes many sports), reads a lot, and likes travelling and regular sessions of profound conversation at the pub. His volunteer pursuits include tutoring immigrant children in preparation for university, and directing daily bouts of 'whiteboard hangman' with roguish gangs of enthusiastic inmates at a seniors' residence. Supposing himself not yet in his dotage he is now attempting to write something other than the academic and technical stuff. He remains guardedly optimistic.

THE PROCESS

Shortlisted story, by Caimh McDonnell

It didn't matter how often he had to go through this, he was a bundle of nerves every time. It's what comes from being beholden to an unfathomable malicious force. Gareth sat on the park bench and tried hard to resist the urge to worry away further at his already badly chewed fingernails. He couldn't remember the last time he'd slept for more than a few hours. He scratched at his raggedy beard with both hands as he let out a growling sigh of frustration. A mother pushing a pram glanced at him with alarm before subtly picking up her pace.

12 days was all it had taken, which anyone will tell you is a ridiculously short amount of time in which to complete a full length novel, even a bad one. Gareth hadn't written a bad one though, no – he'd written a masterpiece. It'd come so easy it felt like he was cheating somehow. As if the book had already been written and he was merely transcribing the words whispered in his ear by a sweet-tempered angel. He'd taken a couple of weeks holiday from the bank and sat in his study for 14 hours a day, typing away. Then like clockwork every evening, he'd go to the gym and have dinner with his family, before drifting into a peaceful sleep, having made tender yet vigorous love to his wife, Samantha.

On the day after he'd finished the novel, he'd re-read it and wept. He'd known straight away what he had done. Humility be damned, this book was going to change lives – his most of all. He rang the bank and said he wouldn't be coming back. He told his boss some home truths about his management style and personal hygiene, then he'd taken Samantha out for a meal at a Michelin starred restaurant. They should start getting used to the good life.

The next day, hung-over but happy he'd walked into his study. It was time to e-mail the finished manuscript to publishers and kick off the inevitable bidding war. He sensed it straight away – something was wrong, very wrong. When you know a room well, you can feel when it has been disturbed – the study felt like it had been violated. It looked just how he had left it the evening before, save for one significant difference. There, propped up on his keyboard was a small rectangle of card with four words printed on it. As Gareth read it, it chilled him to his very core – 'We have your book'.

Frantic, he'd checked his desktop PC, the laptop, his two e-mail accounts, the three data sticks and the wastepaper bin. Everywhere, every last word of the book had disappeared. Gareth forced himself to take a few deep breaths, it didn't matter – it was all still there, inside his head, he'd just write it out again from memory. He sat there for hours staring at the flashing cursor on the screen but nothing would come. The characters that had danced so vividly together across his mind, now tripped and trampled on each other's toes. The previously sweet-tempered angel screeched manic words of unintelligible fury in his ear.

There was a number on the back of the card but first he'd contacted the police and Samantha's cousin, the lawyer. They both said the same thing; seeing as there was no evidence of a break-in and nobody but Gareth had actually read this book, it was his word against whoever's number it was that it had ever even existed. The cops didn't come right out and say it but the message was clear, if you want it back you've got to play ball.

He rang the number. A calm female voice answered, "Hello Gareth."

The first time he tried anger, the voice hadn't engaged, just hung up on him. The second time, he tried pleading and was met with an identical click followed by the dial tone. The third time, he'd said what he knew whoever 'they' were had wanted to hear. "What do I have to do?"

The instructions hadn't made sense but he'd nevertheless followed them to the letter. He'd completed 46 levels on Angry Birds, twirled around in his office chair 3,046 times and spent six hours trying to sketch a portrait of the lesbian songstress KD Lang – from memory, despite having never enjoyed her work. At the end of that week, he'd then been given this location and he'd waited patiently at the allotted time. A man in a long brown Phillip Marlowesque mac had sat down beside him and wordlessly handed him an envelope containing the first four pages of his novel. All attempts to engage the man in conversation had been met with a blank stare.

When he got home he'd rang the number again and received his next set of instructions and on it went. Under orders, he now spent his days getting into arguments on one internet forum advocating passionately for the use of goal-line technology in football, while on another forum, taking the exact opposite stance. He watched every episode of an almost entirely incomprehensible Japanese game show, learned to play the bagpipes – badly, got into a protracted turf war with Mister Patel at number 45 about a perfectly harmless hedgerow. The requests went on and on, each more pointless and futile than the last. Every week he'd do as he was told in exchange for a few paltry pages more.

It was almost two years since it had started and he'd now earned back just over half of his novel while losing almost everything else. Samantha had taken Max and Libby to 'visit her mother', that'd been three months ago now. He'd gone around to visit on Sunday, Max barely said two words to him. As Samantha had closed the front door behind him, he'd stood on the porch with tears in his eyes. In the hallway he heard his sweet Libby talking to her mother.

"Mummy, daddy smells sad."

"I know sweetheart, I know."

Gareth jumped as the man in the mac sat down beside him. It always unnerved him that he seemingly appeared out of nowhere. As usual, the man wordlessly slid an A4 envelope across the bench. He opened it eagerly. "No – there must be some mistake; there's only one page in here. Look!" Gareth held out the solitary page, making no effort to keep the pleading tone from his voice. "It's not even a full one. It's just a couple of paragraphs!"

He was taken aback when for the first time in two years, the man in the mac spoke. "You were told to spend 5 hours a day practising your farmyard animal noises."

"But I did, I did!"

"Do a duck."

Gareth quacked pitifully before the man shook his head in disgust. He was tempted to debate whether a duck really qualified as 'farmyard' but thought better of it, reason had never worked before with these people.

"Also, we told you six months ago to gain 40 pounds."

"I tried but..."

"From now on, every meal will have an ice-cream course."

Gareth nodded wordlessly.

"And stop sneaking out to the gym."

How did they know, how did they always know?

The man stood as if to leave. Gareth could feel tears welling in his eyes, "I'm sorry I, I... I'll cancel my membership!"

The man looked up briefly, as if he was receiving instructions from on high.

"No – leave the direct debit, just stop going."

The man pulled his collar up and began walking away into the soft mid-morning drizzle.

"Wait!"

He stopped and slowly turned his head to look at Gareth.

"Please I... I have to know. Why are you doing this?"

The man's harsh gaze softened at least momentarily, to a look of near pity.

"Because it has to be the same for you, as it is for everybody else."

And then he walked away.

~

Caimh McDonnell's Biography

In his decade on the British stand-up circuit, Caimh McDonnell has firmly established himself as the white-haired Irishman whose name nobody can pronounce. He's also had four critically acclaimed hour-long shows at the Edinburgh fringe.

When not performing stand-up, Caimh is in great demand as a writer for TV. He has recently worked on *The Sarah Millican Television Programme* and *Mock The Week*. He also works as a children's TV writer and was BAFTA nominated for the CBBC animated series *Pet Squad* which he created. He was a winner in the BBC's Northern Laffs sitcom writing competition, where he was lucky enough to be mentored by Craig Cash and Phil Mealey of *Royle Family* fame. He's had a lot of sitcoms optioned by production companies but none have yet to get commissioned, which he is absolutely fine with.

He has only very recently started writing prose, mainly because it was a refreshing change to be able to write something where only his opinion mattered. He lives in Manchester where he is about to start his Masters in Creative Writing at MMU – because the library looks nice.

TO ALLITERATE, FULL STOP

Shortlisted story, by SS Kaye

F

Foundations for Phillip's fame lay with his flamboyant personality, and a feat of fortuitous good fortune with his first play, which focused on Facebook.

Fascinated by his fabulous, fresh-sounding scripts, the stage world fed on his frequent flirtations with faith, filth, fantasy and societal façades.

Financial freedom from student debts unfurled as his fame flourished.

Flowers from fans festooned his home.

"My life is FANTASTIC!" he flushed to infatuated followers during auditions for his forthcoming feature, an affair foretelling fake religious philanthropy entitled *Full Stop*.

U

Sali, an unassuming urban girl, earned the part of Una, the principal lady.

Her understudy was uniformly uncomplicated.

Unctuousness from the director did nothing to undo the utopia underlying its rehearsals.

The play was upholstered with uttermost care, producing scenes of ubiquitous and unrivalled beauty.

L

"LOVELY!" he enthused to Sali. "Your luminosity brings enlightenment and delights the listeners!"

Her lithe, long-limbed frame lay languidly along the chaise longue as he added, "Although your lines can be a little lack-lustre. We need to liven it up, amplify the tempo, make it less lethargic!"

She glared at him through luscious liquid eyes, highlighted by her long lashes.

"I've learned my lines as instructed!" she flashed. "LET me be leisurely. My approach injects elegance and lowers the levels of belligerence."

Phillip leapt lightly on to the stage and leaned against a pillar. Softly he lilted, "A little lecture on attitude, my love. You might be the leading lady but I am the director. LISTEN to me." He glided across and lowered himself to her eye level. "Let's be less of a Lush, please." Lifting her chin with long fingers, he was lost in the lagoon of her languorous look. *"Oh Lord!"* he gasped as their lips locked.

Their love-making was luxuriant and electric.

He lavished her with lust.

She lavished him with love.

The affair lasted weeks until...

L

..."I love you," she lisped.

"Love?" He laughed. "Love is the lament of the lost! You leaden your life with this ludicrousness!"

"But I AM lost without you," she wailed.

"Listen my lovely, you confuse lust with love," he stated. "Do not laden me with your latent idolisation."

"Let's live together. We can be liberated!" She lurched for him. "You love me!"

Lying at his feet she clutched his linen-clad legs; "You recline on your laurels, lauding it over us; leering at the ladies; pretending you don't care. But you long for me!"

"This is laborious and labour-intensive, Sali. You're becoming a leech."

"Live with me! We belong together!" she yelled.

"LEAVE ME ALONE, you lampooning lunatic," he lashed out. "It's time you left! Lily will replace you. She is the new leading lady."

S

The Senior Journalist for *Surety Star* and the supervisor of its press releases sat alongside Phillip, stirring hot soup and slowly slurping the steaming liquid from her silver-plated spoon.

He slid across to her, snatching a surreptitious squint at her short skirt. "So, spill the beans." He smiled. "Share your thoughts, Tasleem; critique *Full Stop*."

She shot a stare of such scorn that he shivered.

"SHAMBOLIC", she sneered. "Anti-Semitic, anti-Sunni, sectarian shite!"

Stiffened on his stool, the tsunami of her contempt showered on his shoulders. "Shame on you!" she shouted. "You've shunned Islam and spurned the sacred scripts of Siddur. You've sold your soul to Satan!"

"Sorry?" he stated. "I don't understand."

A stringent stillness ensued.

"What's your s-s-strategy?" he stuttered.

Stop sabotaging me with your sleazy sentiments and lies, the synapses in his skull screamed. *Your subterfuge will spoil the show!*

She shattered the silence with her statement; "That was my SISTER you sacked, you scumbag," she hissed. "Sali! Your sidekick!"

"Sorry?" He smirked. "Sali is your sister?"

"You've scarred her soul with your supercilious smugness," she spat. "She is severely shaken by your self-satisfaction."

"Listen now, Tasleem, Sali didn't suit the part," he sighed. "She had to be substituted."

"You SLEPT with her, you western scumbag. You abused her. You used her. You shouldn't have done it, you piece of SHIT!"

He started, shocked by her slew of spite. *How does SHE know about the sex?* he speculated. *That slut must have revealed our secret!*

He stared at her snake eyes. "Not sure I know what you mean." Saccharin-sweet sarcasm seeped from his lips as he supposed denial.

"She is suicidal, don't you know?" she shrilled.

"It was just a shag, sweetie! Let's not sensationalise the sex!"

"You SLIMEBALL!" she sneered. "She's Sunni, you're Protestant. And now she's EXPECTING!"

Slander and sleaze enshrouded Phillip as she persisted; "It's an insult to Sali's status. And you will suffer the consequences. I'm stirring a serpent's nest to suffocate and smother you..."

T

Tasleem turned to the internet with the intention of inciting hatred towards Phillip's theatrical transcripts.

Using Twitter and text messages to target terrorist factions, the tentacles of her smear campaign tantalised fanatics with terrible accusations – some tantamount to sedition.

Tensions mounted as the tendrils of her thoughts were translated into tons of tongues.

Phillip was taunted and tormented by multimedia images depicting torture, and intimidated by death threats.

O

Ordinary life for Phillip was obscured by the ominous threats.

Opaque opinions oozed like an oil slick on the internet; opium for the overly obnoxious wishing to obliterate this modern-day Rushdie.

Obloquy from Orthodox Jews led to outlandish outcry in synagogues.

Muslims obstructed the occidental playwright's oratory.

Obsequious observers of the Orange Order, supporting their Protestant outcast, outraged the Christian world.

P

Persecuted by persistent predicaments, permutations of pain perforated Phillip's psyche.

Newspapers reported his production as 'passionately pernicious' and 'prohibitive'.

The Prodigal Prophet Party privately plotted punishments for Phillip's provocative prose.

Preachers of pious populations pissed off politicians put under pressure to place him in a penitentiary.

"These people cannot be permitted to play the part of a pretend Pontius Pilate!" Phillip protested publicly. "I am being persecuted by parasitic fundamentalists pushing for my crucifixion."

Perhaps the project pushed the parameters of politeness, he pained privately.

Panicking, Phillip implored protection from the police, who pontificated before pooh-poohing his pleas, paying passing heed to his plight.

A three-pronged metaphysical pincer opened as the pinnacle approached:

The Prodigal Prophet Party executed their plan to purvey him to perdition, and a parcel packed with phosphorous was posted to Phillip's place.

Sali's parents executed their plan and poured petrol on to Phillip's porch.

Phillip executed his own plan and primed his Walther pistol. Perspiring profusely, he pointed the PPK at his temple.

Phosphorous, petrol and pistol exploded.

Phillip perished.

~

SS Kaye's Biography

Am currently 75,000 words into writing (rather badly, it must be said) a complete pile of drivel that keeps me stressed and entertained and exhausted and exhilarated in equal measures. I have two children aged eight and five who keep me stressed and entertained and exhausted and exhilarated in equal measures, and a husband who used to be a vet and is now a bestselling author who keeps me stressed and... yes, I'm sure you get the point.

Inner Me is obnoxious, Outer Me is kept less interesting so that it can't be categorised with such strong language.

TO HULL AND BACK

Shortlisted story, by Julia Breck-Paterson

"I've been there." Di raised a half-interested eye from her Sudoku and scratched the cat's ear with her pencil. "Weather was lousy."

"What?" Freddie paused from his master-planning of the evening's telly-viewing, thumb hovering over the buttons in selectus-interruptus. "Been where?"

"Hull... and back."

"Who mentioned Hull?"

"You did. Just now. For some reason."

"No, you daft dipstick! I said To *Hell* and Back. It's on tonight, channel three at nine o'clock."

"Oh. I thought you said Hull. Not that there's all that much difference, if memory serves. My lasting impression is of concrete."

"Was that before we—"

"Yes," said Di, hurriedly; propelling her mind speedily over the ghastly pantomime where she and Freddie had first met, *Babes in the Wood and Bold Robin Hood* – a mediocre Victorian throwback, in which Freddie was giving his Will Scarlett and Di was second fiddle to Maid Marion. "Ages before that."

Di wrinkled her brow. If only she'd kept a diary. Ha! A Di-ary! Then she might remember the tour, the play, who was in it... who the heck had she worked with, all those years ago?

The cat, bored with being poked at intermittently with an HB, jumped down and sauntered off to surprise a mouse. Crewe! Crewe station – vast, bleak, and freezing-frigging cold, in the early hours of an autumn morning...

"D'you want to watch it? I think it's about a bloke who ends up bumping off his mother-in-law."

But Di was already on the road to Hull.

*

They'd rehearsed in London under the eagle-eye of a slightly loony, Irish director named Desmond.

The shambolic Desmond had managed to scare some half-decent performances out of his cast, and, as the opening date drew nigh, had promised transport by van to the various outposts of the British Isles, designated by the Arts Council, to be recipients of his oeuvre. Said oeuvre, *Rumpelstiltskin*, junior version, was to be thrust upon unsuspecting pupils of nominated secondary schools, in accordance with the Secretary for Education's big literary push. As Desmond put it, "A planned military movement against the enemy, culture apathy." Di struggled to equate 'culture' with the doings of a greedy miller, his daughter, wicked royals, and a malicious sprite, but gave up, and just took the money. Like many of his countrymen Desmond could be verbose, witty and moody, in turns. He lived on the edge of his nerves and progressed with alarming rapidity from foot-stamping ire, to tearful sentimentality.

On the whole, it was a happy company. Anthea, an eager newcomer, was Desmond's assistant stage manager; a title greatly outweighing its actual status as tea-maker and dogsbody. Bob, a great big bear of affability, jovially un-greedy in real life, made a convincing miller and father to Griselda, played by Faye, a serious Australian girl with a heart-shaped face and high cheekbones, intensely intent on making something of her career. Dark-haired, busty Di, cast as wicked Princess Isabella, practiced being evil whenever she passed a mirror, raising her hairline and narrowing her eyes. Her brother, King Brian, a mild-mannered, moon-faced, bespectacled actor, named Dave, seemed suitably oppressed, in rehearsals, by his royal sibling.

Melissa, tallish and thinnish, was cast as messenger, huntsman, and general extra bods, whilst the eponymous character was played by Janine, a small, slender redhead.

Actually a dancer, she had the height and body of a 12 year-old boy and was therefore perfect as an elfin character, physically, at least. Unfortunately acting was not her forte, but she pranced and gambolled to great effect.

"Someone shut that bloody door!" yelled Bob. "Might as well rehearse on the roof, it's like a wind-tunnel in here."

Desmond tutted and backtracked, trying to kick the door shut behind him with a heel, teetering wildly and almost spilling his two Styrofoam cups of coffee. "Now look," he said, petulantly, "that nearly went on my jacket."

"It didn't, though, did it," muttered Dave, from behind his newspaper. "Anyway, why do you need two coffees?"

"To keep me from dropping off, listening to you lot droning through my brilliant script. That's why," retorted Desmond, waspish, now.

"All right Desmond, don't twist the old pantaloons, duckie," said Bob.

Desmond lodged his coffees safely, pulled himself up to lean, lanky attention, sucked in his cheeks and clapped his hands. "From the top," he called, "and I mean everybody, peasants and fillers-in... we get the cossies tomorrow."

"Ooh, goody–" said Di, loudly, and was quelled by a sombre look from her director.

"Places, everyone, and give it some welly."

During the run-through Desmond paced and waved his arms about, like a demented conductor at the Last Night of The Proms, afraid he was going to miss his bus. "What animal does he remind you of?" said Bob, behind his hand.

"A giraffe on LSD," said Dave.

"Spot on."

"Well, it was better," said the giraffe, at the end,

pushing his hand through his mop of wiry hair, "but notes, notes, people. Gather round."

Di put her hand up, "Desmond, when do we actually open at the National, before or after the schools tour?"

"Very funny, Diana. I'll thank you to note that Young Peoples' Theatre is an important contributor to the future of the arts. These kiddies are theatre-goers in the bud, and you dish them a load of old how's-your-father and they could be lost for life. Who knows what could stir in those tender bosoms – maybe a future Olivier sits in the ranks of your round-eyed audience; thrill and inspire, thrill and inspire!"

"Right," said Di, "not The National, then. Who's getting the benefit of our talents? I'm not going to Upper Volta."

"You'll be OK then, we're doing Milton Keynes, Wolverhampton, Crewe, Hull and back down again."

"O deep joy," said someone.

"Notes," carolled Desmond. "There's only one of you who is the least bit convincing – who actually acts as if they mean it." Six minds preened, thinking, that's me. "And that's Faye. The rest of you should apply to Sainsbury's when the tour is over."

Faye blushed. The rest looked indignant.

"You," Desmond poked a finger at Di, "walk around like a half-shut pen-knife. Boobs out the front and bum out the back, like shelves." He sketched a vertical line on the white-board and endowed it with a pair of triangles, front and back, "See? Straighten up. Bum in, head up. You're meant to be regal, not touting for rides on Clacton sands."

"Ooh," whispered Dave to Bob, "now we've got a giraffe and a donkey."

"What am I?" asked Bob.

Dave thought, "A bear. Me?"

"A mouse. Or a rabbit – no – a mouse. No offence."

"None taken. What about Faye?"

"A cat, definitely."

"Anthea's the rabbit, and–"

"Do you two mind?" called Desmond, clapping again. "Sure, you'll drive me to drink!"

"No, you can walk to the Red Lion, Des; it's only round the corner."

Desmond threw down his script and flounced out of the room, which went quiet before the giggles started, then hushed again as Desmond marched back as though nothing had happened. "Sprite!" He addressed Janine. "All I can say to you, is when in doubt, dance. Now let's go down the pub."

*

The company gathered promptly at 9am the next day, excited starlings at the doors of Berman's theatrical costumiers, to be met and ushered in by their 'giraffe' who turned up in a flapping mac, and in full voice about irresponsible drivers and parking spaces.

"Inner London isn't noted for its parking-friendly environs," Bob pointed out.

"No, but I have to load up the costumes, Robert, I'm not carting half of Berman's back on the tube."

"Point taken," said Bob.

The girls fell on the costume racks like squeaking vultures, supervised by a member of staff to make sure they didn't sully the goods. The place had a special smell, borne on the wings of old velvet, greasepaint, dust: the fragrance of theatres. Although everything was cleaned and kept in good order, the flavour and romance of these costumes hung like intoxicating breath over the souls of the young actors. They felt privileged and suddenly, if briefly, conscious of the path they trod.

Desmond had a list. To be strictly adhered to; budget controlled.

"Two garments for Faye as she has to progress from country girl to queen, one for everybody else, apart from peasant tunics and cloaks. Oh, what am I thinking! Faye can have a tunic for the first act – as you were, and check everything with me before trying on."

Desmond made an adjustment to his list and curled his cupid-bow lips in delight at his inspirational accounting. "Hard luck, Faye," was Dave's heartfelt commiseration. He liked Faye. Lots.

The efficient assistant knew her stuff. "That won't fit you," she said to Di, "besides, pink hardly spells 'wicked' – your character needs drama."

Faye looked perfect in the pink, innocently lovely, whilst Di was guided to a striking number in black and silver. "Ooh, I like it," she said, "very medi-evil," and peering inside the neckline found the original label – 'Olivia – *Twelfth Night* – created for...' and the name of a famous young actress. Oh, to be wearing the gown *she* had worn! Maybe lingering essences of her talent had permeated the velvet and would transfer, by some mystical osmosis, into Diana. "Love this one Desmond." It was approved.

"Can I have a pointy hat to go with it?"

"No, that's extra. You can have a cardboard crown, like the king. They'll look OK from a distance and you can take them off before you go amongst the audience."

"Go amongst the audience?" Di stiffened, shy Faye

went pale, Mel, Bob and Dave looked wary and Jan the sprite frowned. "You mean we have to mingle with the kids, afterwards?"

"Yes."

"They might ask questions."

"That's the idea. You are there to *inspire* them, remember? Explain the meanings behind the play."

"What meanings?" said Dave. "I thought it was a frigging fairy-tale to get them off classes for an afternoon."

Desmond groaned and pushed his hands through his hair again, 'til it resembled a last-season's abandoned bird's nest. "There is a great moral example in *Rumpelstiltskin*, people."

"Better explain it to us before it all hits the fan, then," said Bob. "We wouldn't want to be responsible for the decline in morals of the next generation."

"Later," said Desmond, obviously smelling revolt in the ranks and a pending scene in the costumiers. "Are we all happy with our cossies? Good. That's everything, then," he turned to the assistant, "not forgetting cloaks and tunics."

Cast members were to throw voluminous hessian garments over their other costumes to act as peasants, when not otherwise on-stage, or wrap themselves in cloaks, to appear as courtiers. Desmond was a born time-and-motion practitioner.

With everything booked out and the hampers stowed in the van, the cast headed for the pub for a bite and a beer, before the afternoon costume run-through.

Desmond also utilised himself to the hilt; on the book, plus managing the lighting board and music, with the enthusiastic assistance of Anthea, the probationary-equity-card-holding ASM, on props, thunder-sheet and tabs, and making sure Desmond didn't fall off his stool whilst frantically signalling his latest preferred stage directions, from the wings.

It all went swimmingly, they thought, despite the giraffe plunging into gloom and despair at regular intervals. The miller bragged about his clever daughter's magical powers; the king clapped her in a tower with bundles of straw; the sprite made clandestine visits, and extracted his dreadful promise from poor Griselda, who was on pain of death from his majesty, egged on by the wicked princess; the king made an honest woman of Griselda; much was made of the baby (a composition doll) and the messenger was sent off to discover the name of the dastardly sprite; said sprite danced round a tree, painted on one of the back-cloths, gratuitously blurting out his secret name, and was thus foiled, leaving the royals to live happily-ever-after, except Wicked Princess Isabella, who was mightily miffed that her power had been transferred to the sweet and good Queen Griselda, her aim having been simply to pocket the gold.

"Broadway, here we come!" Bob punched the air.

"Broadmoor, more like," snapped Desmond. "But at least you all remembered your lines."

"Let's settle for all stops to Hull," said Di, flopping onto a chair. "Did my bum look better in this?" she asked Desmond, smoothing the pile of her velvet gown.

*

The tour wasn't half bad, actually. They picked up the enthusiasm from their young audiences and survived the 'post festum' mingling, discovering that children were prepared to believe the cast knew what they were talking about, just because they were bigger. If it didn't make sense they assumed it was their fault, whilst the actor moved swiftly on to the next eager-beaver. Teachers, already stuffed to boredom with literature, only wanted to offer tea and cakes, and ask what they'd been in.

Each new location was scoured for a good chippy, an Indian or Chinese, and a pub that was not possessed of the dimensions of The Albert Hall, whilst Desmond and Anthea checked the venues to decide on the optimum spot for fitting-up – erecting the temporary stage. Even schools that boasted a proper stage still had to suffer the scaffolding that held the back-cloths, wing-cloths and front tabs, or curtains, as the stage management couldn't rush out and operate the big, in-situ stage curtains, between scene changes. Some head-teachers were piqued that their nice stage accoutrements were not to be utilised, but Desmond knew his own mind; even if no one else did.

*

"Oh, isn't he beautiful!" Di sighed. "I think I fancy him."

"Come off it," said Mel, "he's about 12."

"Who cares? Look at him."

They were surveying, through the thin overlap of the front tabs, the sea of pupils seated on the floor of a school hall. The youngsters chattered excitedly, darting expectant looks toward the front, waiting for something to happen. Di had spotted a golden head, slightly above the others, fronted by a face of incredible handsomeness, and fallen in love.

"Yeah, ha-ha," scoffed Mel.

"I could eat him."

"Right. Shall I bring you a file in a cake when you're banged up for running off with a minor?"

"You must admit, he has the face of an angel."

"Yes, and plays football and sets light to his farts and puts beetles down girls' blouses. He's a boy, Di, and as horrible as all his mates."

"My soul longs for beauty. I look at that face and hear the music of the spheres."

"You're either hungry or randy. And since you've had lunch and are thinking about spheres, I imagine it's the latter. You need a good seeing to—"

"I heard that," said Bob, suddenly appearing. "Anything to oblige; your hovel or mine?"

"Geddof, you silly bugger!" laughed Di, "or you'll have me through the curtain."

"That too, if it tickles your fancy."

"In a month of Sundays, Bob. Fumble off!"

They were bored, that was the trouble. The shows were fun, but the rest of the time? Nine weeks on the road and utter ennui. Once they'd seen all the films a town had on offer, at reduced rates upon production of their Equity cards, there was little to do apart from gaze into a beer glass all evening. They weren't even cosy pubs, where you could make silly faces in polished copper jugs, hanging from beams. They were great mausoleums full of fag-pong, red plush, mock leather and loud carpets that didn't show the sick stains.

"Bloody awful," moaned the girls, whilst the chaps played darts or bar-billiards and Desmond sunk deeper into his Irish whiskey.

"Doan worry," lisped their trusty director, waggling a finger, "next stop Hull. You'll love it."

"Can't wait," they said. Oh, the glamour of show-biz!

*

It was raining, of course, which got poor old Hull off to a bad start, and Desmond had stopped the van midst a forest of concrete tower blocks, vehicle-lined streets and walkways with business premises.

"Well, this is a treat, folks," said Di. "Let's all rush out and play in the sand."

"Don't judge," scolded Desmond. "I've rented us a couple of flats, boys in one, girls the other."

"That's not fair," said Jan. "There are more of us."

"Yes, and you have an extra bedroom. Stop griping."

Desmond consulted his map, drove to a higher level of the car-park, and ushered them out. Bob made a facetious joke about it being roomy but sparsely furnished, which everyone ignored, following Desmond through the swing door to the flats.

Like most rentals they smelled of old cooking-fat and dog-ends but were clean enough, though Mel freaked out when a large spider emerged to see what all the vibrations were about.

"I never took you for a cowardy-custard," said Di. "It's only come out to say hello."

"Shit! I don't care. I've been known to move house because of spiders," Mel shrieked. "I can't possibly sleep in a flat with it."

"Pity, I was going to invite you to join us," said Bob. "This is our one; you're next door."

Melissa fled without further ado.

Kitchens inspected, beds sorted, they sallied forth for a scout round and fell into Mario's Pizza Place. Satiated, the boys left first, to find somewhere to play darts, whilst the girls toyed with their coffees and added more lipstick and eye-liner to their faces.

"Well, mine's a gin and tonic," said Di. "Who's coming?"

Whilst rain teemed from gutters into drains, they trekked around the concrete walkways, backing out of the pub where their happy male colleagues were aiming missiles at a dartboard amid loud and rude comments, finally coming to rest at a hostelry that met none of their requirements, except that it sold intoxicating liquor. "Sod it," said Di, "I can't go another step in these heels, I've got blisters. The only thing you can say for this shite-hole is that it's undercover."

Clutching their drinks they found a table and plonked round it. Di looked up.

"Ho-lee Hell," she said slowly. "Or should that be Holy Hull...? Look what I spy."

Gazing at them intently from two tables away was as fine a group of masculine specimens as they'd seen in a long time.

"Fucking manna from Heaven!" said Mel.

Anthea, Sprite and Faye just ogled. Everybody broke into smiles.

"They might be mass murderers," said Anthea.

"We'll take our chances," said Di and Mel.

The mass murderers virtually sprinted across, vaulting chairs, coming to rest at odd angles; one with his bum in the air and both elbows on the table, one kneeling on the floor, chin in his hand as he peered at Faye, one slid down the bench to rest beside Mel, another twirled a chair and sat on it, back to front, gazing at Di. They were all grinning.

Di's one said, "Marry us, we're dying."

The testosterone could have been counted in layers.

These were not local lads. These were quite obviously beings of their own species; everything about them proclaimed it.

"We're a fit-up company on a school's tour," said Spritie. "We've been nine weeks on the road and we're cheesed off."

"We are doing *Julius Caesar* at the New Theatre; been here six weeks and are growing hairs on our palms."

"What?"

"Never mind. We were all on the verge of suicide. In fact, making a pact this very evening – then you all walked in. Let's celebrate!"

Mark, Mike, Tom, Steve and Tony suddenly made the concrete jungle glow. Even the grey, stained walls and iron grilles of the flats seemed less gross.

Non matinée days and Sundays were given over to outings, when they heaved themselves up from whatever bed they'd spent the night in.

The boys knew of an amazingly tiny pub, run by a little old lady, from her own home in Beverley. They drove out in Tom's van, with the boys singing a bawdy song the girls had never heard.

"I don't want to be a soldier,

"I don't want to go to war.

"I'd rather stay at home,

"Around the streets to roam,

"And live off the earnings of a lady typist..."

They thought it was hilarious and insisted on learning it, bawling it out from the tops of their lungs on every outing in the van, relishing the final verse and collapsing with mirth.

"I don't want a bayonet in my belly,

"I don't want my bollocks shot away,

"I'd rather stay in England,

"In merrie, merrie England,

"And fornicate me bleedin' life away-ay-ay."

"Jeez, that's funny," said Di.

"Yes, it is," said Tom. "Sad to think it was sung by those poor buggers in the Great War, who really meant it. Sobering"

*

Their final stint in Hull was a convent. The delightful nuns couldn't have been kinder and the first half went like a dream. Then the devil took Di, who decided to make additions to the doll posing as the baby Rumpelstiltskin was trying to get his grubby little mitts on. With her eyebrow pencil she applied spots, round glasses and a moustache to its face, and nearly corpsed as she handed the bundle to Faye, with the words, "Take her my dear, she's lovely."

Faye swayed slightly, delivered her line and exited, followed by Di, where they instantly collapsed, snorting into anything that would muffle their helpless laughter from the audience. One by one the others peered over to see what was up, and fell into the same state, even Desmond, who was the first to pull himself together and realise that the stage had been empty too long. They got back on track by a masterpiece of control, until Rumpelstiltskin pranced up to the tree and said, "My name is..." and Bob, behind the backcloth said, in a sing-song voice, just loud enough for Spritie to hear through the fabric, "Crumpledforeskin."

Obviously the nuns hadn't heard Spritie say, "Fuck off," in an undertone, nor the gurgles of uncontrollable mirth from backstage, because everyone clapped loudly and they had a splendid tea, with Sister Benedicta's home-made scones.

That evening, Desmond, having taken more whiskey and less coffee in his 'coffee', all day, and not stinted on the bevvies in the pub, staggered out at closing time and was deeply offended that no one wanted a lift home.

"We'll get a taxi, Desmond. Leave the van where it is – you can't possibly drive it."

A full-blown tantrum ensued. His Irish blood was up; his manhood impugned. No one could prevent him stomping off into the night. 20 minutes later their taxi pulled up beside a forlorn Desmond, standing by a ditch, alongside the white, upturned, bulk of the van. "It wouldn't have happened if you'd been with me," he wailed.

They bundled him into the taxi and left the van to be recovered the following day, without recourse to the local bobbies.

The next day a teachers' strike was announced, spelling the end of the line for *Rumpelstiltskin*. Fond goodbyes were said, telephone numbers exchanged, and Di found herself waiting for a connection, in the early hours, on the bleak wilderness of a Crewe platform.

One of the boys, Mark, from *Julius Caesar*, had made it big. She'd continued to see Tom when he turned up in London, but, well, a 'fling' on tour, is a 'fling' on tour. Funny, but until that evening she'd thought Mel was gay. She'd encountered Spritie again, strangely enough, in Egypt, looking dead glamorous, in a nightclub dancing troupe. Small world.

"D'you want to watch it, then?" asked Freddie. "It's not a murder, it's a war film with Audie Murphy."

"Yeah, OK."

On reflection, the road to Hull hadn't been all bad.

~

Julia Breck-Paterson's Biography

I was born on the Isle of Wight in 1941, when my father was serving in the Royal Navy, based on Culver Cliff.

I was an art student and a commercial artist, venturing into acting – theatre and television – and working many years with Spike Milligan.

I moved to France twenty-five years ago and returned to art. I paint, make miniatures and write, having a couple of novels on the go. My entries to the To Hull & Back comp have not been published or offered anywhere.

I joined a creative writing group and we published a volume called 'Every Other Friday', in which I have several short stories and nonsense verse.

I am married, with three sons, scattered far and wide. Have two dogs and a cat and like condensed milk.

I really have been to Hull.

I would like to write more, but the comp closes in seven minutes.

And I have noticed that all my sentences begin with I. Sorry!

JUDGES' STORIES

ANY OLD IRON

Judge's story, by Steph Minns

Grandad's specialities were stories from his youth, which he delighted in telling us every other Sunday when we visited. Grandad would sit, enshrined by cushions and wrapped up in his favourite brown cardigan with the wooden toggle buttons, for all the world like an enthroned king overseeing his court. He had to look his best for us, he always joked, shrewd blue eyes twinkling as he warmed up to his tale, playing us, his audience.

"Geezer must 'ave been an old bloke back then," he began. My small sisters fought over the 'front row' cushions and quickly settled. Being the oldest at 14 I had the sofa privilege.

"He looked ancient to us kids anyway, an odd fella with long silver hair, always wearing an old funeral director's coat and a battered top hat with a pheasant's tail stuck in the band. Tall 'n' skinny, looked a bit like a scarecrow. He was a rag 'n' bone man, that's what they called them that went collecting junk. Don't know why 'cause they didn't collect bones, just scrap metal, old pans, old clothes – that was the rags. "Any old iron," he used t' shout, 'cept you couldn't make out the words as it all came out like one nonsense word 'cause 'e said it so quick. He had an 'orse called Boo who used t' pull the old flatbed cart, up an' down Walthamstow High Street, past the market, up 'n' down the streets, past the station. Diesel trains had come in then but there were still steam engines in the railway sidings, used to shunt freight.

"Proper East Ender was Geezer, liked his beer and a sing-along around the piano in the George on a Friday night. No one used his real name, jus' called 'im Geezer, 'n' us kids of the neighbourhood doted on his every word. He was a bit of a mystery. No one seemed to know where he'd come from, if 'e had brothers 'n' sisters, if he'd ever been married. He had a scrap yard just behind the railway sidings, lived there with his 'orse.

"I got a look in there once. Geezer invited me 'n' Tommy Ashford in. Like a treasure trove it was, stacked with books, old lamps, chairs, all sorts of antiques. Once 'e kidded us 'e had a genies' lamp. He got out an old bashed up oil lamp and rubbed it, muttering some mumbo jumbo, telling us the genie would pop out. 'Course we believed 'im. Bet our faces were a picture when smoke started drifting from the spout! It was just a lit fag he'd hidden in there to kid us. He was good at tricks an' illusions an' always had a new one t' show us."

"What colour was Boo, Grandad? Did you ride him?" my pony-mad littlest sister piped up.

Grandad paused to reach for a digestive from the plate Mum offered.

"Black 'n' white, patches all over. Proper gypsy cob Boo was. No we didn't ride 'im. Boo was a workin' 'orse. That was 'is life, up an' down the streets pullin' the cart."

"Oh Dad, don't tell them any more about that weird old man," Mum tutted. "You'll give them nightmares."

"Nah, they love it," Grandad chuckled. "All kids love scary tales an' this is a special one 'cause it's true."

"True!" Mum snorted. "I remember you telling me he put a live spider in his mouth once to scare you all. Made me shudder."

Grandad threw back his head and laughed, his scrawny turkey neck jiggling up and down as he crowed at the ceiling. Wiping tears from his eyes, he carried on.

"Yeah, old Geezer. He swallered it too, crunched it all up in his gappy teeth, shnacketty shnack, and jiggled his tongue at us to show it was gone."

Grandad mimicked the action and a chorus of, "Urr, Grandad," went up from us.

Mum left the room to start tea and that gave Grandad the opportunity to relaunch into this Sunday's tale. He leaned forward to get our attention, not that he needed to as we were all ears as usual.

"Now, I was 12 years old that summer, 1947, just after the war. I used to hang out with some kids the same age on the streets after school and on a Saturday, when we'd often see Geezer on his round, shouting 'any old iron' 'n' ringing his hand bell. Boo plodded along, knew his route by heart. Our mums sometimes gave us apples for Boo and old stuff for Geezer, which he accepted graciously as though they'd offered him gold necklaces and not worn pots and broken knives. 'It's all treasure, lads,' 'e said once, showing us a bashed enamelled cup he'd picked up earlier as though it were a king's chalice or some such. He made it all special, tellin' us stories about the things 'e'd come across. 'You can find magic in ordinary things with a bit of imagination,' 'e always said, and I reckon we were all convinced about that.

"So when kids started vanishing we trusted Geezer, believed his tales. First was my mate, Tommy. Never came back from the corner shop. I knew 'im well and all the parents went out combin' the streets, police 'n' all. But there was no trace of Tommy. It was as though he'd vanished into thin air. A fortnight after he'd gone missin', Geezer pulled up on 'is cart and took a book out of 'is coat, beckoned us over all secretive like. Tommy's been taken by goblins, 'e said, see here 'e is trapped in the picture in this book.

"We all crowded round to look and, sure enough on page 96, there's a picture of a little blond haired boy, cryin', tryin' to escape from the clutches of five 'orrible goblins. I can see that picture now, the boy wearing brown trousers and a blue shirt, just like Tommy often wore. The old cover of the book had a tea stain the shape of a rabbit on it. *Mr Farley's Bumper Book of Fairytales* it was called. I can still see it to this day. There was a picture of a witch on a broomstick on the front, the tea stain covering her left foot.

"But here's the creepy bit, Tommy appeared again a week after Geezer showed us the book. Police found 'im wandering in a daze in Whitechapel market, miles away, and all he would say was Geezer saved 'im, rescued 'im from the goblins by bursting into the cavern where they'd imprisoned 'im. His parents took 'im away to live somewhere else shortly after that 'n' we never did get a chance to ask Tommy what 'ad happened. We heard the adults just supposed whatever had gone on had disturbed 'im so much 'e made up the goblin bit and Geezer part to explain things for himself, try an' block out what really happened.

"Except Geezer showed us the book again, and this time there was no little blond boy wearing Tommy's clothes, no little boy in any picture with goblins at all in fact. Me 'n' Jimmy Cook asked if we could look through it 'n' we spent an hour goin' through every page, twice, tryin' t' catch Geezer out. There were no pictures on page 96, and none of the stories had anything t' do with goblins kidnappin' boys. But it was the same book, with the witch 'n' the rabbit tea stain on the cover."

Grandad sat back, nodding with satisfaction and we all gawped at each other. My smallest sister had saucer eyes. This was a good story indeed. He carried on.

"Geezer told us there was a bogeyman hunting kids t' eat in the East End. We didn't want t' believe him, but how could we not after that? Then a second kid went missing, Jack Hargreave, and again the police knocking door to door, frantic parents all helpin' look for 'im in the park, by the river, on the common and along the railway. Not a sign of 'im. Geezer turns up with a seashell and gets us all to listen to it, hold it to our ear. We all fancied we could hear Jack calling for help in it, as well as the sea. Geezer said this one would be harder as 'e was far, far away, down on the coast in Essex. He reckoned 'e could see Jack in his mind, trapped in a deserted boatyard, fed on by the bogeyman but still alive. He showed us Jack's yo-yo, said he'd dropped it as he'd been snatched and holdin' this let Geezer see where our mate was. I knew it was Jack's as it had 'is name on it in green pen – I'd watched 'im write it, proud and careful, when he'd bought the yo-yo.

"Well, word got to one of the parents that Geezer 'ad Jack's yo-yo. It'd been in 'is pocket apparently when he'd gone missin'. My dad heard talk down the pub that some parents at the school were gettin' suspicious of Geezer, what with 'im always hanging around the kids an' givin' us things, just small things like tin cars or puzzles he'd picked up in a house clearance or summat. Tommy goin' on about 'im bein' there an' saving 'im didn't help none and after the third boy went missing just two streets away, that same month, the police hauled the old rag 'n' bone man into custody."

Mum came in to check the time just then, interrupting Grandad's flow. She'd obviously overheard the last bit and, curiosity stirred, she sat down on the arm of the sofa next to me, prompting.

"So what did happen to him, Dad? Was he charged with kidnapping the children?"

"Well, no. They 'ad nothin' on 'im. Police went through 'is lock up, turned it right over and made a fine mess. All they found was junk. Police roughed up poor old Geezer too, we heard whispered on the street. Seems they treated 'im as though 'e was guilty of being a pervert anyway, even without a trial."

Mum looked uncomfortable and shooed the girls off to the bathroom to wash their hands for tea. I, being older, was allowed to hear the rest of the story. Grandad continued in a more subdued, thoughtful manner, no longer playing for a young audience.

"Y' know, Rosie," he looked at my mother. "Geezer was alright. I'm sure 'e didn't do nothin' bad to kids. He just liked amusing us, seein' us laugh, and especially the poorer kids who 'ad nothing. He'd fix up broken dolls and tin fire engines that had been dumped, fix 'em in his workshop and just give 'em to kids who had no toys. Boy, you should have seen the faces of them poor kids. Geezer was magic to them, Father Christmas all year round."

Mum nodded sympathetically.

"After the third kid vanished Geezer was beaten up badly. I 'eard Dad tell Mum he was lucky there hadn't been enough blokes in the neighbourhood with the gumption t' form a lynch mob. They all thought he'd had a hand in it somewhere, y' see. Dad reckoned 'e took kids to order for some mob in Whitechapel. That's where they'd found Tommy, gibbering.

"Geezer 'ad some weird stuff in 'is lock up. He showed me that time I went there an old handwritten book covered in yellow waxy parchment. He said it was a witch's spell book. Covered in human skin 'e said it was and 'e used it to help him trace the kids."

"Oh Dad! You believed him?"

Mum stood up, having heard enough it seemed.

Grandad stiffened and looked away.

"Well we were just kids," he muttered defensively.

I waited until she'd gone back into the kitchen to shell the boiled eggs before I pressed Grandad further.

"So what became of Geezer then? Did you ever find out?"

Grandad stretched in his cardigan, flicking biscuit crumbs from his lap as he recovered his composure.

"I saw 'im one last time, coupla years later. He was livin' rough down on Leyton High Road in an empty shop. Beggin' on the street 'e was, beggin'! That proud old man that 'ad once 'ad 'is own business. The way he'd been treated 'ad broken 'im. I sat with 'im for a bit, bought 'im some food an' talked while I waited for me bus. After he'd been threatened his landlord 'ad chucked 'im out and sold Boo, but Geezer never saw any of the money from 'is 'orse. All 'is stuff was just burned or dumped. He wasn't allowed or daren't go back for fear of 'is life 'cause everyone thought 'e was guilty. It was a sad thing t' see 'im like that. I felt bad about it and went back that winter t' find 'im, maybe 'elp 'im. I asked around but local shopkeepers said he'd died, alone in that freezing, derelict shop at the end of the street."

Grandad fell silent then, pressing his lips together in a tight line at the memory. I noticed his hands were shaking and he seemed suddenly very old, like an orange that had had all the juice sucked out of it until just a tired old shrivelled skin remained.

"'Ere lad, come out the back with me. Don't tell y' mum about this or she'll 'ave me certified."

I dutifully followed him out to the lean-to, not much more than a timber frame covered in mildewing corrugated plastic sheet. Grandad's shuffling slippers left a snail-trail through the dust on the concrete floor. A Central Line tube train rushed past at the end of the garden, headed for Leytonstone station, sending the rails singing and splitting the tranquillity of the evening. Once it had passed we could hear each other speak again.

"Here."

Grandad lifted a carefully bubble-wrapped object out of a wooden banana box on the peeling shelves. Curiously, I unwrapped it to find a palm sized, slightly battered conch shell. I was studying biology at school so recognised it immediately.

"Put it to your ear," he instructed, his face serious. "What d' you hear?"

"Our science teacher told us it's just ambient background noise resonating in the shell. Everyone likes to think it's the sea they hear though." I replied.

"Is that all you can hear?"

Grandad had become suddenly intense, watching my face like he watched the horse racing on TV when he had a bet on.

I shrugged but then I heard a small far-away cry. It sounded like a young boy sobbing, "Help, please help me." I held the shell away from my ear, listening intently, assuming it was a kid shouting nearby on the street. But I heard no kids playing nearby, just the drone of cars.

Rain started to splot onto the corrugated plastic above my head and I tried the shell again. This time I was sure I heard that boy cry, "Geezer! I know you're here – help me!"

Unnerved, I shoved the shell quickly back to Grandad. My face must have given the game away. Grandad nodded solemnly, frowning.

"So you can hear 'im too. It's Jack, still trapped there. That day I saw Geezer sleepin' rough 'e gave me the shell, begged me t' take it in return for the food I'd bought him. I've 'eard that voice ever since. Not every time I listen, but most times. All through the years Jack's voice 'as haunted me through that shell."

He looked drained, desperate, grey. I was lost for an answer, lost for anything to say.

Mum called, "Tea's ready," at that moment and I was glad of an excuse to go back into the house, unsure what to make of this. An old man, losing his marbles? Grandad sighed, muttering.

"I keep hoping one day I'll hear Geezer in there too and know everything for Jack will be alright, that he's free. I keep listenin' an' hopin' that Geezer can sort it out, wherever 'e is now. If anyone could do it 'e would."

During the car journey home, Mum tried a little probing.

"You're quiet, Josh. What were you and Grandad talking about in the lean-to?"

"Just stuff," I mumbled.

My pony-mad sister interrupted. "Do you think Geezer really knew magic, proper magic like Grandad said?"

"Yeah, I think he did," I replied quietly.

~

Steph Minns' Biography

I've been a keen reader, writer and artist since childhood. Originally from the suburbs of London, but now living in Bristol, UK, I work part time as an administrator and spend my spare time writing. My dark tales range from stories set in dystopian realities to ghost and horror.

My publishing history to date runs to six short stories.

Horror short 'Bloody Christmas' is to appear in Grinning Skull Publishing's seasonal horror story collection Christmas 2014.

Horror short 'Tiny Claws' won the *Dark Tales* March 2014 international competition and is due out in a winners collection in 2014.

Dystopian tale 'Dreg Town' is due to be published in 2014 in an anthology by Almond Press, called *Broken Worlds*.

Gothic ghost novella *The Tale of Storm Raven* was published as an e-book by Dark Alley Press in April 2014.

Dark fantasy 'The Flight of Horses' appeared in the sixth *Darker Times* horror fiction anthology after receiving an honourable mention in their November 2013 competition.

Ghost story *Watcher from the Woods* was published as an e-book by Alfiedog Publishing, August 2012.

Steph's website: www.stephminns.weebly.com

~

Steph's Competition Judging Comments

This was a tall order as the shortlist was so good. All had elements that really grabbed me and made me think about issues such as what constitutes a good ending. To pick a number one was certainly a challenge.

DEATH OF A SUPERHERO

Judge's story, by Christopher Fielden

"Name?"

"Batman."

Death looked up from where he was seated on the Throne of Bones, behind the Desk of Deliverance, in front of Death's Door. Although dressed like Batman, the person standing before him didn't exhibit the level of physical fitness you might expect to see from a successful crime fighting vigilante. For one thing, there was an unacceptable disparity between their height and girth. Said disparity would probably make leaping from buildings, running quickly or fitting into the Batmobile somewhat problematic. The person also seemed to possess a general lack of understanding regarding Batman's gender.

"Nice suit," said Death.

"Thanks."

Batman obviously had no concept of sarcasm either.

Death looked back at his Recent Expirees' Manifest. He tapped the page with a bony finger.

"You're listed here as Doris Claymore," he said.

"Never heard of her," said Batman.

Death reached out and stroked the decaying blade of the scythe that rested against his desk. "This is quite simple, Doris. To progress peacefully into the afterlife, you need to confirm your name. It means I can be certain of who you are, what you've achieved in life and, therefore, where you should spend eternity." Death dished out his best glare. As glares go, it was pretty impressive. In the past, it'd made stars think twice about shooting. "Can you tell me your real name please?"

"Already told you. I'm Batman."

"How can I put this politely?"

"No need to be polite," said Bat-Doris. "Got skin as thick as armadillos, us crime fighters."

Given the invite, Death decided to be blunt. "Not only is Batman fictional, *he*..." Death left a pause which he hoped would scream with meaning, "...is a man."

"And?"

"You have breasts."

"They're pecs."

"No, they're breasts," said Death, "and Lycra does little to mask their magnitude. I feel I should add that

Batman was always depicted as an athletic individual, at the peak of physical fitness. Clearly, you're not."

A tear trickled from beneath Doris's mask, suggesting her skin might not be as thick as she'd led Death to believe. "OK," she whispered, "point taken."

Despite the scythe, the rotting cloak and the distinct lack of flesh coating his crumbling bones, Death was a sensitive individual. He disliked causing upset. Most people found the experience of dying traumatic enough, without him being disagreeable.

In a more gentle tone, he said, "Good. What's your real name?"

"Bruce Wayne."

Death took a moment. His was the greatest of jobs, an eternal vocation no other would ever undertake. The pride he felt in this most trusted position was indescribable, the honour overwhelming. Still, on certain days the downsides of immortality became glaringly apparent and he realised how lucky mortals were to die. This was one of them.

"You're not Bruce Wayne," said Death, deciding it was time to unleash some even harder truths. "Or Batman. Your name is Doris Claymore and in life you were a fat, frumpy nurse."

Another tear appeared beneath the mask and trickled down Doris's chubby cheek. Death felt guilty. He'd allowed irritation to control his words, creating insults when he should be showing more respect. Eternal life would be dull without the challenges people like Doris presented.

One of the lessons he'd learned by existing for as long as things had been dying was the art of patience. It would be a shame to forget that lesson today. There would be a reason why Doris was behaving in this manner. It was Death's duty to discover the reason and deal with it. He decided to try a different tack.

"How did you die, Doris?"

"I was doing some vigilante stuff, you know, chasing a psycho across rooftops, that kind of thing."

"And?"

"I did a jump from one building to another. And missed."

Given that Doris probably had a bodily mass similar to that of a rhino, it wasn't hard to imagine gravity prevailing while she battled with thrust, momentum, distance and the laws of physics.

"That's exactly what I have written here," said Death.

"See, I'm telling the truth."

"Next to the name Doris Claymore."

"Must be a typo."

"It also says that you were at a superhero convention, had a Jagerbomb or 17…" Death paused and double-checked the number, "…a Jagerbomb or 17 too many and got a bit carried away. Does that sound familiar, Doris?"

"Stop calling me Doris."

A tremble in Doris's voice caused Death to look carefully at the woman standing before him. Fear danced in her eyes and she kept glancing over his shoulder.

"It's the door, isn't it?" asked Death.

Doris nodded.

Death's Door was huge and set into a wall of light behind the Desk of Deliverance. The portal was sinister, black and fleshy. Blood oozed from its surface, which gave the impression the door might be alive, but only just. Death often wished he could alter its appearance, and the foul smell that emanated from it, but there were always barriers to major changes in the Realm Beyond Life, including politics, beings who believed they were gods, the dead's expectations and laws dictating The Way Things Should Be. Sometimes it was easier not to bother.

"It's going to judge me, send me to hell," said Doris.

"Judgement is my job," Death replied, "and there's no such place as hell."

"You said what I've done in life tells you where I should spend eternity."

"I did."

"I haven't done anything." Doris looked at the door again. "Well, I've done plenty, but none of it was much use."

"And Batman did lots of good things, right?"

Doris nodded. "I'm going to a bad place, aren't I?"

Death looked back at his notes. "You were a nurse in a children's hospital, working on the cancer ward. It says here that you were good with children. You could put them at ease, even in the most difficult of circumstances."

"Anyone can do that."

Death shook his skull. "It's a difficult thing to do. I can see why you sought escapism by drinking and playing superheroes. But you were gifted. You did a great deal of good with your life. You helped others."

"Lots of people help others."

"True. But you – you were better at it than Batman."

A smile crept onto Doris's lips. "You're good at this."

"Thank you," said Death.

Doris pulled off her mask. "Sorry if I was difficult."

Death saw that all the tension had left her. She looked radiant and, more importantly, ready to state her title.

"What is your name?" asked Death.

"Doris Claymore."

Death stood, hefted the scythe and tapped it against the door. There was an unpleasant squishing sound. Fresh blood oozed from the door's surface. As if this meant some toll had been paid, the portal swung open, revealing Doris's pathway – a glimmering road that led through stars and galaxies towards the Ever.

"This is your path beyond life, Doris Claymore," said Death. "May it bring you peace."

Doris stepped through the doorway and embraced eternity. The door shut behind her. Death rested his scythe against the desk and sat on his throne.

"Next," he said, looking through the manifest, trying to find his place.

He heard some shuffling footsteps.

Without looking up, he said, "Name?"

"Wonder Woman," replied a gruff voice.

"For fuck's sake," said Death.

~

Christopher Fielden's Biography

When I left school, I decided to play drums in a rock band, much to the joy of my parents. I did this for 15 years. It was a lot of fun. The band did not make me a millionaire.

After the band split up, I started writing fiction. I self-published my first book *Wicked Game* in 2010. To avoid a mental breakdown, I then started writing short stories as they're a lot easier to finish. My stories have been published in print and online by many fine publications, including *Writers' Forum*, *Scribble*, *Writers' Village*, *InkTears*, *Brighton COW*, *Darker Times*, *World City Stories* and *Little House Creative Workshops*.

Next year, *InkTears* will be publishing 'Death of a Superhero' and four other of my short stories in a showcase collection alongside some stories from a few other fine authors. This makes me very happy.

By day my job is in digital marketing, where I spend most of my time trying to avoid wearing a suit. By night I play drums in a multitude of rock bands, including Ye Gods! and AD/HD. In between, I ride motorcycles, write and run my website.

Chris's website: www.christopherfielden.com

~

Chris's Competition Judging Comments

The 2014 competition received 94 entries. It was incredibly hard to select the shortlist and winners because there were so many amazing stories entered. Honestly. I'm not just saying it to be nice. It was a pleasure to read so many fantastically inventive tales, all containing elements of pure writing-magic. I'd like to thank everyone who entered.

If you entered the competition and didn't make the shortlist or receive a special mention, please don't be disheartened. Many of the stories entered into this year's competition were very, VERY publishable. Just because you didn't make the shortlist does not mean you won't succeed in the future. Every judge's scoring system and opinion is different. Please, keep submitting your stories elsewhere.

Overall the competition made a small loss. Why? Because of competition advertising costs, design costs, prize money (this year, first prize is £100, second prize is £50 and third prize is £25), Paypal charges, video production costs, costs associated with publishing the anthology and, of course, the loooong ride to Hull and back.

Despite the loss, I've decided to take a gamble (assuming I'll sell a few copies of this anthology) and double the prize pot for next year. In the future, I'd love to be able to offer the winning writers thousands of pounds. That's the aim. So I intend to up the prize money on offer every year if I can.

I'm pleased to say that I didn't have to disqualify any of the entries into this year's competition. The majority of the writers obeyed all the rules. A few made minor errors. To keep things fair, part of the scoring was based on obeying the rules, so if anyone did make an error they received a lower score during the judging process.

It was very interesting to see the scores from the different judges. Each of us had different tastes and a wide variety of stories from the shortlist were deemed winners. In the end, the stories that won were those that continually scored well across the board. It just goes to show, judges opinions do vary, so if you don't succeed in one competition, keep entering others. You *will* be published eventually.

There's not much else to say really. I laughed a lot while reading the entries, and that's something I like to do. I hope everyone who has purchased the anthology giggles a lot too.

THE MAGNIFICENT ESCAPE OF BERYL BIGSBY

Judge's story, by Christie Cluett

Beryl Bigsby had formulated another escape plan. She wasn't sure if it would work this time, but she was determined to try because she refused to die in here. On the other side she imagined walking down the street with the sun on her face, heading wherever she wanted, to see whoever she wanted; hopefully a man with hips like a snake-oil salesman and eyebrows that suggested he knew how to make a woman's knees go weak.

"Beryl, do you want to play Majong?"

Beryl looked up at Gladys Emsworth, whose cardigan buttons were done up wrong, and cracked the arthritis in her fingers.

"Piss off, Gladys," she said and stood up. Slowly. Beryl had turned 92 last week and so she did everything slowly, but no matter how long it took, she was going to get out of this home if it was the last thing she did.

"Beryl! Beryl!"

She groaned, tugged her surgical stockings higher and started shuffling out of the social room. A man with a full head of white hair, wearing a tie and a pastel blue jumper, tottered after her.

"Go away, Sid," Beryl hissed over her shoulder.

"Beryl, I just wondered if you'd like to have dinner together tonight. You could have my jam sponge?"

"We always eat dinner together. Everyone eats dinner together… every day. Go away. You're going to give me away." Beryl flicked her eyes first left then right, before leaning round the corner. The coast was clear.

"You'll only get caught again. Why don't we sit together at bingo? You could use my dabber," he said, combing his hair back into its pristine side parting with his hand.

Beryl looked back, a scowl on her face. "Sid, if I have to play bingo one more time I will do me, you and everyone around us a serious injury with your dabber."

Sid nodded, taking a moment to think about it, while Beryl returned to her surveillance of the corridor. At the far end, where the junction turned left and right to the residents' room, was a large laundry basket on wheels. It was full to brimming with white towels and sheets. Beryl listened for a moment and then, satisfied, she hefted up her stockings again and hobbled at a more urgent pace towards that basket and her freedom.

She passed the TV room a few moments later with a

determined look on her face that was morphing into a gurn. In an effort to go faster than her cankles would let her, she leaned forwards into the position of a champion downhill skier as she moved past the kitchen. Eventually she reached the laundry basket, gripping the edge for support as she caught her breath. She narrowed her eyes, wiped the sweat from her face and raised one slippered foot. It wavered half a metre or so above the ground for a second or two, before Beryl gave up any hope of just hopping in. Instead she tried the tactic of just leaning against the side and hoping for the best.

For a moment she thought the plan had failed as her hip met the basket, but momentum took her and as her top half fell into the basket so her feet followed. She heard Sid gasp from behind her as she vanished into the laundry, and smiled as she pulled the sheets over to cover her. She gasped herself as she remembered where she was and whose sheets and towels she'd just drawn across her face. Beryl breathed shallowly and reminded herself that this was her Shawshank Redemption.

10 minutes later, after she'd shooed Sid away twice, the basket began to move, pushed by unseen hands. Beryl suppressed a giggle, ignoring the fact that her knees felt like they would never unfold again, and thought about what the sky would look like once she was free.

*

Beryl was sat with knitting on her lap and her arms crossed, refusing to join in. A male care worker was smiling at her.

"Roger, I will rip that smile off your face and use it to wipe my shoes if you carry on in this manner."

"Oh, Beryl!" Roger said, with a chuckle, dismissing her words with a swat of his large hand. He then placed it on his padded hip and sauntered away. The other residents were making cards for various relatives, who only came to visit once they'd forgotten about the smell. Beryl watched them with a scowl, concocting a new escape plan in her head. The laundry basket hadn't been wheeled onto a van and driven outside the gates as she'd been expecting. Instead it was wheeled to a room of washing machines at the back of the residence that Beryl hadn't seen before. When Roger had peeled back the top sheet to reveal her slumped in an awkward position, he'd sighed, chuckled and wondered off to get some assistance.

"Beryl?"

She looked up. Sid had something in his hands.

"What?"

"I made you a card," he said, offering her a flowery mess that smelled of glue and unfulfilled dreams.

Beryl just stared at him, her arms still crossed, so Sid opened it himself.

"I'll read it for you, shall I? Roses are red. Violets are blue. You like steamed kidney pudding. And I do too."

"Jesus Christ, Sid. Jesus Christ."

Beryl thought about getting up and managed it not that long after. Sid edged his way back to the table, to further hone his poem, while Beryl slipped a knitting needle into her pocket and made for the door.

*

Beryl was remembering or day-dreaming, or both; who

could be sure after all these years. In the faraway magical place of the past she had long blonde hair and wore colourful dresses that twirled when she spun. Her shoes were dainty and her ankles thin. Her skin was unmarked, unwrinkled, and she wore an expression that held no trace of the years to come.

Beryl blinked away the sights and sounds of her youth and looked down at her fingers; knobbly fingers that were trying to slot the knitting needle into the keyhole of the office. She glanced down the empty corridor and then up at the 'Private' sign that hung above her head. She smirked at it and thought, not for long. As she poked the knitting needle above, below, around and anywhere but in the keyhole, she ran through her plan: pick the lock, enter the office and shut the door. Rush to the desk and search the drawers for the cash box. Break it open and stuff the money into the pockets of her cardigan, and her slacks if the amount warranted it. Check the coast is clear and run to the hall to hide behind the coat-stand. Wait until 11.15am, when the doorbell would ring, as it did every Tuesday, and the grocery delivery would arrive. Wait until Roger opens the door, push over the coat-stand and escape in the resulting chaos.

Beryl looked at her watch, 10.57am. The dance of the knitting needle increased in tempo and then suddenly she thought she heard a faint click. She tried the handle and, with a smile that would light up a room, she was through.

10 minutes later Beryl was standing behind the coat-stand with 11 pounds and 43 pence in her pocket and a whole lot of hope in her heart. She tried not to breathe as the minutes ticked by, tried not to think about where she would be, what she could do in only a few minutes.

At 11.17am she started to worry; the doorbell still hadn't rung. At 11.23am, she could hear Roger chuckling as he walked by.

"It's Thursday, Beryl," he called.

At 11.43am Beryl came out, her head weighed down by yet another defeat, and walked slowly to her room.

*

The next day, Beryl was sitting staring off into the distance with a dabber in her hand. Sid sat next to her with a grin that his face couldn't contain. He smoothed down his side-parting and passed Beryl her stack of bingo cards.

"See? This is nice, isn't it? What could be outside that could be better than this?" Sid sighed happily and waited with his dabber poised as Gladys turned the handle of the machine the wrong way.

Beryl said nothing, just stared at the numbers in front of her.

"Stairway to heaven, number 11," Gladys called from the front, putting the ball in her pocket.

Beryl, eyes still down, slowly moved her dabber and pressed it onto a square on one card, then another and another.

"You missed one!" Sid said, happily, pointing and nodding at a card by her elbow.

Beryl didn't say a word but dabbed at the card with tears in her eyes. Sid's smile faltered for a second.

"Staying alive, 85," Gladys said, staring at the ball before starting to laugh. She continued while the rest of the room looked down at their bingo cards in silence. Sid looked at Beryl, her head down and the fight gone, and wondered how to cheer her up.

"Do you want to have dinner together today, Beryl? You could have my Spotted Dick?"

Beryl didn't smile, or shout, but nodded instead. Finally she'd said, "Yes," but Sid didn't feel as happy as he'd thought he would.

*

Later that day, Beryl was standing on the roof of the old people's home, looking up at the sky and then down at the ground. Her slippers were peeking over the edge of the wall where she was standing precariously in the wind. She didn't want to die in there, amongst the smell of over-cooked cabbage and subsequent flatulence. She breathed in the afternoon air deeply and rocked forward slightly on the balls of her feet. If she was going to die here, it would be on her own terms. She looked down at the grass three stories below and hoped it wouldn't hurt.

"Beryl!" Sid's voice was out of breath. She could hear the rattle in his throat as he tried to walk and talk at the same time. She looked back and saw one liver-spotted hand reach up to the top of the ladder. Sometime later his white hair poked over the top, flapping in the wind.

"Beryl, wait!"

Beryl sighed and hoped her last moments weren't going to be taken up with another one of Sid's poems. He continued to struggle onto the roof, minutes ticking by, until Beryl noticed the bundle of white he was dragging up with him. She turned slightly, intrigued and her foot slipped from the top of the wall. Beryl fell backwards and landed with a bump on the roof behind. She sat stunned for a moment and then began to cry, big heaving sobs that shook her shoulders and her tight white curls.

"Beryl! Beryl, don't cry. Please. I've brought you a parachute," Sid said.

Beryl looked up surprised and blinked, her face puffy. Sid held up the white bundle and Beryl could now see what it really was: sheets, both plastic and cotton, dressings and bandages all tied together into a canopy with surgical stockings for a harness.

"I had to steal the key to the supplies cupboard from Roger, but the man's an idiot," Sid said. "If you want to be free, Beryl, you should be free. You can fly away."

Beryl looked at Sid with her mouth open for a while. Then she smiled and wiped away her tears and let Sid help her into the harness, their arthritic fingers fumbling together. Quite a while later Beryl was suited up and stood once more on the edge of the roof, ready to jump. This time Sid was holding up her parachute and she was smiling.

"Maybe you'll come back one day and say hello, Beryl? You could have my Wet Nelly?" Sid was shouting behind her, above the wind, but Beryl wasn't really listening. She was looking at the sky and wondering what it would look like on the other side. Then she put one slippered foot out and jumped.

Epilogue

Who knows what the sky looked like to Beryl as she jumped, if it felt like freedom as she sailed through the air. Who knows what she was thinking as she fell towards the ground, or how she felt when the wind caught the canopy of care home supplies and lifted her up above the gate. Who knows if she was happy as her slippers sailed over the gate, clinging onto the surgical stockings on either side. Who knows what freedom felt like when she finally got it, just before she collided with a tree and broke her neck. But what we do know is that Beryl Bigsby died with a smile on her face, knowing what the sky looked like on the other side.

~

Christie Cluett's Biography

Christie is one of the founding members of Stokes Croft Writers. She writes humorous fiction and is currently finishing her first novel, a dark comedy about a Geography teacher's breakdown. In the meantime, to keep her hands busy and get the weird images out of her head, she writes short stories about the odd characters that fill her dreams.

She lives in Bristol with her husband and their 6 happy, healthy chilli plants, trying to convince the former to buy her a sense room and to remember to water the latter.

Christie's website: www.christiecluett.co.uk

~

Christie's Competition Judging Comments

In preparation for this, I made sure to judge lots of people in my everyday life. It didn't go down very well with my nearest and dearest and I still found choosing a winner extremely difficult. It was an honour to read other people's words and witticisms and it almost didn't feel fair to have to choose only one. However life isn't fair so we did.

Well done to everyone who entered – it was a joy – and to Chris for starting such an excellent competition. Have fun in Hull!

THE SPIRITUAL SPROUT

Judge's story, by Carrie Breeze

Man. Life is good!

I'm getting closer to my destiny every day now. I just know it.

For as long as I can remember I've been training for this moment. It's so close now all my senses are alive.

When I was growing up I could feel the strength of the seed, even though there was no notion of where I was heading.

The seed turned into a strong shoot and I started to wake up to a deep knowing of what I needed to do.

I started to look after myself really well. Keeping hydrated, taking a nutrient rich diet and spending all my time in the great outdoors.

This made me grow ever stronger and with it came the sense of knowing why I'm here.

Oh, and how I love the seasons. The sun! The rain! To be one with Mother Nature as I ground myself in her soil.

Winter is here now and I can hardly contain my excitement any longer. I know the moment is upon me. This is it!

*

What's it all about. Heave myself out of bed. That was a waste of time. Hmph. Shove some cardboard cereal down my throat. Coffee doesn't do it for me anymore. Wet cold three minute walk to the bus stop. Can't even be bothered to listen to my iPod. No one will notice they are all just a bunch of zombie robots anyway. What a trudge. 30 minutes on this rickety germ infested steamed up bus to go and spend a day being bored out of my tiny brain. How did this happen.

*

Today I travelled from Brussels to Seattle, an uncontrollable urge to take flight; I had no choice over the destination, I simply had to go.

I arrived at Pike Place Market, a must see for all visitors to Seattle.

Oh! The colours. The smells. The sights. The sounds. I'm bursting with life, energy and excitement.

I'm living the dream!

*

Will this day week year ever end. Boring. Tedious. Monotonous. Tiresome. Mundane. Dull. Humdrum. I only do this job as I don't know what else to do with my miserable existence. And to top it all Christmas. It's all everyone talks about. Trying to outdo each other with their stupid little table decorations. And if I hear one more thing about a personalised cracker idea for Uncle Ted I am going to go over there on the day and ram Uncle Ted's cracker right up his...

*

Oooh, I love this market!

I've found me an awesome spot to hang out and can see all the comings and goings around me.

The hustle!

The bustle!

*

Trudging. Again. Smelly overcrowded overstocked market. Hmph. What's that commotion going on over there. Well I am not rubber necking like the rest of these money driven oooh its Christmas and I must spend all the money that I don't have on stupid expensive produce and flashy table napkins so I can tell everyone how fabulous I am idiots. Not me. I am not part of the crowd. I'll go round the other way and with a bit of luck it will all be cleared up and over by the time I get to the veg stall. Hmph.

*

Hey! What was that? It feels like, like, the root of my being has been severed from whence it has always been.

Woah! Argh! I'm falling! I've been separated from my stalk, my roots. What's going on?

Phew! It's OK, I've been training and am well on-form to take on anything that comes my way!

I love new experiences! I learn from them! I soak them up and allow them to make me grow.

In fact, the market roof looks pretty cool from down here!

*

Humans. All the same. All that commotion. I can't see anything going on here at all and it was only 10 minutes ago there was a huge fuss. Attention seeking make a mountain out of a molehill low lifes.

*

Uh oh. What's that shadow coming towards me? It's like a big... a big shoe.

Ouch!

What's it all about?

*

Woah. I am sliding. Perfect, my day is getting better and better. Hmph.

Oh I'm on the floor. I must've banged my head. Look at that, I slid all the way down the aisle on just one sprout. Ha! Ha! Hey, the roof looks pretty cool from down here! It's OK, I'm up. All is well! No harm done!

What a ride! Oooh, I love Christmas! Now, what shall I have for tea? I am starving! Man. Life is good!

~

Carrie Breeze's Biography

I like to write stories from the imagination of my 12 year old self, although I am a teensy weensy bit older now, I have more life experience to experiment with!

The Spiritual Sprout is based on a true event where I once coasted the entire length of a Sainsbury's aisle on an individual sprout. Shortly after this life-changing incident I went travelling for the very first time and many journeys have followed since.

Carrie Breeze is my pseudonym in which I write ditties, short stories and all things silly. Carrie does not have a website but you can find her on Facebook.

Georgie Fielden is the girl behind Carrie who enjoys adventure. Georgie has travelled extensively and her real passion is cycle touring. She will be sharing a new adventure blog of her mammoth cycle ride through the African continent with the Ubuntu Cycle – www.theubuntucycle.wordpress.com – which is due to start October 2015.

In the meantime both Carrie and Georgie are hiding away in Deepest Darkest Devon. Carrie is turning her shed into a beech hut and Georgie is cycle training.

Georgie's website:
www.georgiecycle.wordpress.com

~

Carrie's Competition Judging Comments

A wonderful agglomeration of hilarity, quirk, wit and imagination unfolded before my eyes as I read through the shortlisted stories, often laughing out loud.

I can see in my mind's eye each individual author busying away at their respective work stations; were they writing at home, in an office, in the shed, at the local café or up a mountain? As they exercise their incredulous imaginations I wonder about the conception of their story ideas.

To think of the amount of hours that must have been collectively spent to bring this anthology alive is mind-blowing.

The scoring system we used helped me to judge each entry fairly whilst allowing for my personal favourites to show through.

I take my hat off to Chris for all of his hard work in creating his website to help and inspire writers all over the world. As to how he managed to make the time to read ALL the entries and whittle them down to a shortlist of just 20 is a true feat of dedication.

It has been a privilege and a pleasure to help judge this unique competition and I am excited to watch it expand and grow over the coming years.

TO THE GRAVE

Judge's story, by Josh Keeling

Hunter Guntridge's grave had been dug as soon as he'd heard about the terminal bowel cancer. They'd given him a year, which was plenty of time. While the church had refused to dig a space for a living person his own estate had acres worth of prime grave-digging soil. So, while declining all professional medical help, he'd instead had a coffin built to fit.

When Hunter felt that he was near enough to the end he had his three, unquestioning maids transport him to the largest tree in the first field. There, hooked up to his own, stolen, life-support system, they prepared him for what was to come. In the shade of the oak his coffin had been lowered into a six-foot pit, now he too was lowered in. Relieved of all duty, the maids just left him to it.

From the grave Hunter made several phone calls to a select group of men he knew from his time spent north of the Thames, each of which he started like so, "You'll never guess where I am."

And nobody did.

Harry and the boys arrived within the hour, they'd always run like clockwork. Though, none of them had really been quite ready for the sight of him waving up at them from a hole in the ground, his face all gaunt and ghostly. They sat for a moment, the five of them, silent, and dangled their legs into the hole, dirt falling onto Hunter's body.

"I suppose you're wondering why I brought you here," he said smugly, "And if you're not, then piss off."

They all laughed duly. Ha-ha-ha. Now they were here though, however confused they were, he knew what they wanted, were expecting, as part of a final payment for their services. The house, the cars, the furnishings and any other left overs. It was a shame that they wouldn't be getting any of it, they'd got enough. By the sight of them, this collection of retired men dressed up like a scene from *Reservoir Dogs*, they'd spent it wisely too. No, that was all for the orphans. Hunter assumed that orphans were still in requirement of large donations from anonymous sources, so the boys would be getting something else. Hunter had a promise that he'd made to himself and it needed keeping.

"Richie, you first. I want to tell you somefin'." The

others stood up out of respect and made their way over to the wall on the far left. Looking up at the ever thin Richie, the dying man was strangely warmed by the way he'd be seeing him off. Over the six decades in which he'd been living, even since birth, Hunter had been a collector. Now it was time to let go of his collection.

Gathering secrets, he'd obtained each with the solemn promise that he'd take them with him to the grave. And there he was. He told Richie this, and then told him what he needed to know, a secret most personal. Afterwards the man stood, bowed and wished him a pleasant death, before walking off to get Gus.

Then Gus sat too, his bulging frame suiting a name that was round enough to fit. The man had wrinkles now, and his many chins were an old man's, not simply a force of majesty. Afterwards the youngest of the lot, Pope, appeared at the far right corner, and soon it was Hitch, both the short-arse and the Italian gave their goodbyes and now only Harry was left.

Harry, his 'executive director', was the only one who'd still come round to see him every few months or so. Hunter had never married, and not wanted to. He knew he was far too selfish for all that. So, sat at the end of his deathbed for the longest, Harry talked of old times and new, and how strangely silent the boys were being.

Soon, having listened intently to Hunter's words, Harry nodded. He got why the silence had fallen so soundly. Pulling a white handkerchief from his pocket, the last one to see him off, Harry let it float down into the coffin. This was the real goodbye to it all.

Hunter reached out to his side and clutched the dove of white fabric. It was as though he'd be able to die now, but not until the fallout. For what Richie knew concerned Harry, while what Gus knew concerned Richie, and Pope's knowledge had Gus involved you see, whereas what Hitch knew centred around Pope, and Hitch was now a new man to Harry. Their silence was pensive; boiling with the childish tears of their wounded pride. Hunter breathed it in through whatever he was breathing with and sighed. It was brilliant. There'd been nights on which each of the respective men's wives had slept with the one whose identity Hunter had been the one to reveal. A base secret, yes, but a secret nonetheless. That was why they were all so quiet. Any minute he expected things would kick off. A standoff, a duel, some fireworks. He'd be going out with a show. Any minute.

The field stayed silent, and disappointed, Hunter soon had to accept that two other possible outcomes existed. On one hand neither of them had the guts or guile to say, in that instant, and this emotional moment, what they now knew. They'd all walked back to their cars and driven off with their fists clenched. Fair enough. Or perhaps they'd discussed it like the gentleman they were. Harry certainly seemed to have matured and the angle he could put on things, like the fact that they'd all been a guilty party, may just have saved any bloodshed. Good on them. Good on Harry, for being a pacifist like that. It had been a long time and what reason would they have for getting truly mad at each other? It wasn't as though they'd told Hunter about it themselves anyway.

Hunter had slept with each of their wives, and each had told him how much more of an exciting man he was than either their husband or any previous member of the group, any cicisbeo at all in fact. He'd learned that word, 'cicisbeo', from Hitch's wife, they were Italian. It was a word for the male equivalent of a mistress. He liked that. It curled around his lips with a smile as he said it from his grave, and his heavy, old east-Londoner's accent gave it grit.

"Chi-chis-beyo, my old man, chi-chis-beyo."

*

Those words were the last words that Hunter Guntridge ever spoke. From above him £10,000 of unplugged hospital machinery fell into his coffin and crushed his major organs before even a scream had left his lungs. 'Fell' was the word the five of them agreed on in the end, it sounded more accidental than 'propelled itself'. Harry and the boys filled in the hole, for legal reasons, and went to choose what parts of old Hunter Guntridge's estate they'd be taking home in their new cars. This was one terrible accident that each of them would each be taking to the grave, all slightly richer for it.

~

Josh Keeling's Biography

A young man with a lot to offer, (only 17, isn't he pretty), Joshua enjoys writing, drawing and long walks in the park. When he's not in his bedroom, practising for the hermit of the year competition, he's outside walking, in a park. Joshua's past achievements include publication by the Young Poetry Network. With a novel, film scripts, poetry collections and an upcoming exhibition in the works, Joshua is not ready to let his lack of any reputation hold him back. Joshua Keeling, one of the talents of the moment that's really worth keeping an eye on, unless you've got something better to do, which you probably have.

~

Josh's Competition Judging Comments

Reading the work intensively and being allowed to rate things by preference was great, normally that's a thing that I can't bring myself to do because I'm just the nicest person in the world since Jesus of Nazareth was around putting his feet in various places in ancient times. To be able to 'judge' showed me what I like, what I don't like and what a brilliant amount of writers there are that have nothing to do with being massively popular and well known (yet, of course) producing content with patterns of thought in line with my own favourites. An eye-opener, more than just for the fact that my eyes were required for the task.

WHEN THE WOODCUTTER'S AWAY

Judge's story, by Leah Eades

When I first took the job up north, the agency said to me, "Bill, are you sure? There's a lot of freaky goings-on up there. All those dark woods and wide open plains attract all the weirdoes and wildlife at once." But of course, I took no notice.

Well, the terrible weather and rural isolation I could've dealt with. Even the darkness of the winter days, where months would pass without the sun ever fully rising, I could've stood. The wife had sent me a SAD light, after all, which I set down by my rocking chair in my bare log cabin and used to light the crossword. *Four-down, six letters: not large. Eight-across, three letters: the colour of rage. Eleven-across, six letters: a Yorkshireman on a horse. Nine-down, four letters: preferred attire of a delinquent.* Hmmm.

What I hadn't signed up for though – what no one had bloody warned me about – were the wolves.

Today was a typical example. All morning I worked hard chopping wood. The snow came up to my waist. All around, the forest was full of glittering eyes and snatches of movement as wolves slipped through the trees, watching and waiting. They know when it's my lunch hour, you see.

I don't know why I bother. I didn't get five minutes down the path towards the village before, predictably enough, I heard the same old screaming. Oh, I wanted to ignore it alright. Let them sort out their own problems for once, that'd teach them a lesson. But I couldn't. I don't know, I guess I'm soft. So, just like I do every other day, I turned around and headed back up the path the way I'd come, with my axe in my hands and a rumble in my stomach that grew louder with each step, and begrudging thoughts of my piping hot dinner going cold at the inn, not to mention the flask of mulled cider and flirtatious smile of Marnie the barmaid going to waste besides.

I headed straight to the place where I knew the screaming was coming from: the Woodside Older Persons Community Cabins, a retirement settlement built for no good reason in the middle of nowhere. Why they don't have proper security is beyond me; I can see from their swimming pool and their golf club that they're not short on cash, and I know how much these kind of places cost. I'd looked at sending my old mum to one myself in her later years, but couldn't even rustle up enough to put down a deposit. What's the price of hiring a few armed security guards, or even just putting up an electric fence, compared with losing paying customers every damned day? It's poor business sense, that's what it is.

Now something softer and lower replaced the screaming. I crept closer to the polished log cabins where the seniors sheltered, careful for my footsteps to not make a sound. I realised it was the sound of a child moaning in fear.

Well, that did it for me, it really did. It's bad enough when those wolves are targeting the pensioners – but when there's a kiddy involved? I'm a father myself, and there are some things a man can't be standing for.

I rounded a corner fast, and came into sight of the cabin – the door smashed, the splintered wood creaking on its hinges. A howl cracked through the icy air. Inch by inch, I edged closer to the doorway and peeked inside.

The scene that met my eyes was as horrible as I'd expected. A small child, a boy hidden within the recesses of a navy blue hoodie, cowered in a corner, eyes squeezed tight shut. All around him, the remnants of a fruit basket lay strewn about, and grapes and oranges exploded beneath the enormous feet of the wolf, who tottered over them on his hind legs, seven feet high, teeth gleaming, and donning an extravagant flowery hat while he admired his reflection in a mirror. He didn't even hear me enter, so entranced was he by his own reflection. I felt sick to my stomach as I watched him sashay, strike a pose and then actually vogue.

The beast was not satisfied though. He turned, with a snarl, to the pile of clothes on the bed – he'd obviously cleared out the wardrobe – which I now realised, to my horror, concealed the granny who lived here. She struggled to escape from beneath the mountain of clothes, and as I watched I saw a frail hand break out from the layers of furs and wools and wave an unmistakable middle finger at the wolf.

The wolf reached down and, with claws so sharp they could slash a man open with a single swipe, hovered for a second before picking up a white silk gown from the heap.

"Oh no you don't!" came a cry from within the clothes, and petticoats and blouses tumbled to the floor as an irate old face burst to the surface. "That's my wedding dress, that is! Get your filthy mitts off of it, or I'll–"

Before he'd got it halfway over his head, the bodice was torn to shreds. Stuck halfway in and halfway out of the gown, he let out a mighty howl that I knew would have his friends come running to help him out. Now was my time to act. I burst into the room, axe raised high, and stood before him.

"You wolves are sick," I said. "Preying on old ladies and ruining their wedding dresses."

The wolf looked back at me and growled, "I just want to look pret–" but I cut his head off before he could finish the sentence.

After that there was the usual clean up: calming down the old lady (this one was a real firecracker). Wiping the eyes of the traumatised child. Apologising over and over again that I couldn't have saved the wedding dress from being splattered with bloodstains during the decapitation. Placing the head of the wolf on a spike as a warning to his brethren. And filing a complaint *yet again* with the retirement community management.

"Sheltered housing?" I said. "What exactly is 'sheltered' about housing a load of frail old grannies and granddads right next to a roving gang of cross-dressing wolves? This is the third intrusion I've had to stop this week. Yesterday one of them made off with an old dear's brassiere."

Of course they smiled and thanked me through gritted teeth and promised that the matter would be raised at their annual board of trustees meeting the following month, but I've been around long enough to know what hot-air sounds like.

And, just as it is every other day, by the time all was said and done, my lunch hour had been and gone and I had to get back to my woodcutting, and work an extra half hour late to make up for it all besides. My stomach wouldn't stop grumbling the entire afternoon.

I'm thinking of contacting the union about this, I honestly am. All the money in the world isn't worth living in a constant state of damn-near starvation. And it's not just me. I've spoken to several of the other guys about this, and they've all been affected likewise. And that one lady woodcutter, the local lass, Little Red – although she isn't exactly little, not with muscles like *that* – told me she even had a run-in with one of those perverted wolves herself when she was a youngun'. She still seems pissed off about it too.

~

Leah Eades' Biography

Leah is a Bristol-based writer originally hailing from the dark hills of Derbyshire. She says she enjoys cycling and running, but really devotes most of her spare time to watching cat videos, drinking tea and pretending to write while secretly listening to musicals. She particularly recommends *Rent*.

Mostly Leah writes short stories, often inspired by overheard snatches of conversation. Choose your words carefully should you find yourself wandering the streets of Bristol, particularly St Pauls.

To learn more about Leah or read samples of her work, you can follow her on Twitter via @LeahEades

Leah's website: www.leaheades.com

~

Leah's Competition Judging Comments

Wow – I take my hat off to all the writers who made the shortlist. It was a privilege to read all of your different stories. In addition to the high levels of originality and writing skill, I was amazed by the diversity, both in terms of style and substance, of what was sent in.

Trying to choose a winner was like trying to pick a Ben & Jerry's ice-cream flavour: overwhelming, and made no less easy by the fact that you know every single one is worthy of your notice. Unlike choosing a Ben & Jerry's flavour, however, I could not be greedy and just eat everything and make everyone a winner. Proof that judging is kinder on the waistline, but harsher on the soul.

A massive congrats to everyone involved: writers, judges, and of course Chris for organising it all. I look forward to seeing the finished anthology – and to hearing about Chris' epic journey to Hull and back....

ZOMBIES ON A BOAT

Judge's story, by Mel Ciavucco

"To summarise today's class, some simple do's and don'ts..."

Her arm flaps as she writes her list of rules on the board. I can almost feel a breeze from her bingo wings. Her hair is the colour things go when they've had bleach spilt on them. It's like she's actually *tried* to dye her hair ginger, not that I know why anyone in their right mind would do that. I hate her. Why the fuck did I let Mum talk me into doing this stupid writing course?

My mop-head tutor continues, "Remember, keep those sentences short and snappy." She's wearing an orange dress over trousers, just to add insult to injury. Doesn't even look like she's bothered to wash her face; she's still got eye crust. "Beware of clichés and stereotypes, and use your '–ly' words sparingly."

Oh God, will this ever be over? It's only one day a week but it feels like an eternity. I'm dying for a cigarette.

"Please never, ever, start sentences with 'and', 'so', 'but', or 'because'. It's a pet hate of mine. Grammatical errors and spelling mistakes are unacceptable of course."

She sets our homework; to write a story of up to 1,000 words on the theme of 'boats' to be read aloud in next week's class. How fucking pathetic. I'm definitely not showing up for *that*.

*

Five minutes later I'm outside sucking eagerly on my long over-due cigarette.

"I'll look forward to your masterpiece on my desk next week then?" Ginger-minge says.

Yes, I often do refer to her as that, not that I can bear the thought of her great flapping fiery haven. "Whatever."

She stops next to me for a moment, clutching a messy pile of papers, her oversized handbag slipping off her shoulder. I should help her but I'm not going to.

"You know, this isn't school, Zandie. You don't have to be here. Why don't you just stay at home next week? Do the whole class a favour."

I blow smoke in her face and she coughs.

"We don't need people like you disrupting our class" she continues. "These people are intellectuals, they like literature and art and, well... they're not drop-outs who sponge off their mum and dad..."

"I don't have a dad. He's dead," I state, playing the guilt card. I always love playing that one.

She rolls her eyes. "Don't waste my time. I don't have time for school kids." She trudges away chuntering something about how it's meant to be a centre for *mature* students, fumbling for her car keys.

"I have no intention of wasting your time," I say walking behind her. "I'm going to write you a story you'll just *love*."

She opens her car door and throws the paperwork on the passenger seat. I flash her a big, forced, toothy grin. She mutters, "Brat," under her breath and slams the door.

I walk off in the opposite direction. Ideas for stories start pouring into my mind. Maybe I will show up next week after all.

*

Zombies on a Boat

SOooooo, there was once a sleepy little iland called Rottnest, in western australia, and there were some were some weird little animals which shat a lot called quokkas, which look kind of like if a kangaroo shagged a possum. And there is a ferry that takes all the rich stupid tourists to and from Rottnest Island, and one day an english family got on the ferry with they're 10 year old son. It was sunny, oviously, it's always bloody sunny in Australia. The crew was typical loud young Aussies. They made an anouncement to welcome the pasenngers and set off on their journey. All of a sudden, suddenly someone saw something brown and fury suddenly running across the floor under a chair, suddenly. The son, who had seen it, said "look mum there's a quokka on the ferry"

The Mum nodded distantly, whilst a crew person who went to get a broom and was tryin to get it out from under the chair. The quokka suddenly leaped out and snarled at the crew member. There was crussty blood in its fur over its face. The quokka suddenly jumped on the mans face, nawing at his nose and everyone started screaming. The man, who's nose was barely hanging on by a thread of skin with blood pourin down his shirt saying "crew', started shakeing and grunting, and his eyes budlged so much that eventually they popped out and hung like droopy testicles.

Another crew member came along and said "Ay Bruce, Gidday, you alright mate?" in his strong aussie accent, but Bruce lunged towards the man and tore a chunk of his cheek with his fingernails and then ate it and then licked his lips sucking up the blood dribbling down his chin and then burped. Then the other crew man started grunting cuz he too was turning into a zombie and then he pounced on the dad of the family.

'Wait, you can't kill me, I have a family! I have a son...' he gurgled as the man pushes the bottle in his throat. He draged it across and the dads blood went everywhere and the mum screamed. The kids eyes widened in the biggest amount of fear he had ever felt. The man cut open the dads belly and started chewing on his intestines...

*

"Get out of my class, Alexandra!" the ginger witch says, not even allowing me to finish reading it aloud.

"It's *Zandie*," I correct her.

She shoots me a look of pure contempt. "Get out."

A few people in the class look as if their pet cat has just presented them with a dead bird.

I grab my coat, scarf and bag. "My fucking pleasure!" I slam the door behind me.

*

At home, my teenage brother, Ben, is hogging the computer as always. I glance at the screen expecting to see the usual array of tits and arses, but as I look closer I realise it is in fact my story he's reading.

"Oh, not watching porn for once?" I say.

He ignores me and keeps reading. He laughs.

"Did I give you permission to read that?"

"It's actually pretty funny. I think we should post it online."

"How about no," I state. "It's just a stupid story, I only wrote it as a joke to piss off my tutor."

He continues reading for a moment until he reaches the end and bursts into fits of laughter. "Oh we have to post it, come on! Let's do it now. I know this website where people read and comment on your stories and stuff and people have gotten, like, famous from putting stories on there."

"Whatever," I say, patting my pockets feeling for my cigarettes. "I'm off. Do what you like. Nobody reads the shit on those websites anyway."

*

"Mummy whats hapenning?" the kid cried. *Mum just screamed more as she watched the guts of the dad being eaten by the crew member, him 'mmm-ing' and 'aaahhh-ing' with every mouthful of intestin. The quokkas continued to attack people, and then those people attacked other people, the boat filling with guts and blood and nobody could escape from the zombies cuz they were on a boat.*

"Mum come on lets hide" the son said and they ran down the ferry away from the screams and the smell of blood and piss. The boy stopped dead. There was suddenly another quokka and it was right in front of him snarling. Mum screamed again.

'maybe if we stay really still he won't see us and will go on by..." the boy was interuppted by the quokka charging at his head and ripping it clean off his shoulders. The quokka smashed the head open on a table and eagerly ate the brains as if he were a starvin Ethopian child. Another quokka suddenly appeared and they faught over the brains and eventually just humped on top of the severed head instead. The mum was frozen in shock, watchin the quokkas fuck each other and her sons severed head and then she puked up and then the quokkas ate that too.

*

"Hey Zand," Ben calls as I try to sneak past him at the computer in the hallway.

I need a lie down. Four pints at lunch time is never a good idea.

"What?" I groan.

"You know I posted your story last week? Well, it looks like loads of people have been reading it."

I peer towards the screen, trying to keep my distance from him so he doesn't smell beer on my breath. He'll only run off and tell Mum, and then she won't give me any money anymore. Ben scrolls down through a long list of comments; mostly complimentary, but also many from disgruntled losers who have nothing better to do than leave pedantic comments on the internet.

"Woah, I never expected so many people to read it," I say. "Budge off it a mo, I need to check my emails."

He gets up still clicking away at the mouse before minimising his screen. He stands to the side of me obviously intent on not letting me use *his* computer for long.

I log in and notice an email labelled 'urgent' from the Rottnest Island Authority.

"Hmmm, what's this?" I mutter. Ben looks over my shoulder. I skim through the email. "...seen your work online... we object to the inaccurate portrayal of quokkas... serious damage to tourism... blah blah..."

I delete it, along with the other junk mail and sign out.

"Why aren't you going to reply?" Ben says, slipping back in front of the computer as soon as I move.

"Can't be arsed. Said I'd meet my mate down the pub."

"It seems kind of important..."

I'm already out the front door.

*

So, everyone on the boat was going crazy and screaming and all grossly bloody and screaming scarily and terrifyingly and lots-of-other-words-ending-in-ly-y but there was one man who could save them all. He was big and black and was on holiday from his work at the NYPD. He was a karaty black-belt and he punched and kicked and karaty-chopped all the zombies and all the zombie quokkas but they kept getting back up again cuz they were zombies so they couldn't be killed. Then he said, in his bad-ass raspy voice "bring it on you furry mother-fuckers!"

The quokka-zombies and the people-zombies all attacked him at once, ripping his lims off his body. A quokka jumped on his groin, tore a hole in his trousers and started eating his foreskin. Another quokka crawled inside the back of his trousers and started niblling his bum. The man screamed a lot and then he stopped because he was dead. And there was no hope for the rest of them cuz the zombies kept eating. The mum watched sobbing wondrin how they will ever get out, who could posibbly save them now?!!!!!!

And then I woke up.
The End.

*

"Gidday. Is that Zandie?"

"Yeah, who's this?"

There is a slight delay. "I'm calling from the Rottnest island Authority, in Western Australia."

"Oh. Rather expensive phone call for you isn't it?"

"Well, it's a very important matter."

"Oh?"

"Your story..."

"Yeah?"

"'Zombies on a Boat'?"

"Yeah. What about it?"

"We would like you to remove it from the internet immediately. The damage your story is causing to our island is irreparable."

"What's that got to do with me?"

"Erm... well, you wrote it."

"So? It was only a joke. Anyway, I didn't even post it online, it was my dickhead brother."

"So you won't mind removing it then?"

"Why? This is stupid. It's just a fucking story."

"Please don't swear at me, miss."

"Who the hell are you calling *miss*?"

The voice is increasingly exasperated. "If you do not remove it immediately we will be forced to take legal action."

"Don't be stupid. It's only a bloody story. What you gonna do, sue me?"

"Yes. That is exactly what we intend to do."

"Fuck off." I hang up. They can't possibly sue me over a work of fiction, it's ridiculous. I need to find my cigarettes.

*

Over the next week I get several more emails from the Rottnest Island Authority.

"It has been a week since we spoke and 'Zombies on a Boat' has still not been removed from the website. We are now taking legal action..."

Blah blah. They can't do fuck all about it. I skim the rest; lawyers, payments for damages to tourism etc. I delete them all. Now they don't exist anymore. I go and smoke a joint out of my bedroom window and then douse the room with a liberal spray of deodorant afterwards. My phone beeps; my mate says it's beer o'clock. Agreed.

*

On my return, Mum is sitting at the kitchen table with her glasses perched on her nose. She takes a deep breath as I walk in. She's going to start ranting at me about something again, I can tell.

She's holding a letter. "Who are the Rottnest Island Authority and why are they suing us for 50,000 Australian dollars?"

"I dunno," I shrug.

"What do you mean you *dunno*?" she says flapping the letter around. "Then why did I have a man on the phone this morning saying he spoke to you a few weeks ago about a story you posted on the internet, and you told him to *F-off*? Is this true?"

It looks as if a vein is about to explode out of her forehead.

"Yeah. So?"

"You can't just run away this time, Zandie. You have to deal with this and learn to be responsible for once–"

The phone rings. Saved by the bell.

Mum runs for the phone. I follow her into the lounge.

"It's for you," she says thrusting the phone towards me. "You can sort this out yourself. I am no longer picking up the pieces for you."

"Hello?" I say. I nod and turn away from Mum's disapproving glare as I listen. "Hmm, yeah OK. Cool. Yeah count me in."

I hang up. Mum stares at me with raised eyebrows. "Well?"

I sit down silently at the table, my legs quivering in

shock.

"Who was that?" Mum asks.

I try to absorb the words I've just heard and breathe deeply.

"Stop being so melodramatic, Zandie," she says sitting next to me at the table.

The words from the voice on the phone repeat over and over in my head. *We loved 'Zombie's on a Boat'! It's going to be huge!*

"I only wrote it as a joke," I stutter. I start to laugh; I'm not sure what else to do.

Mum seems to be looking at me with a little more concern, as if I've gone mad. "What is this story you've written anyway?"

"Just some silly zombie story..." My laughing dies down. "I can't believe it. I really can't believe it."

"Will you just tell me what this is all about?"

"That was a film producer on the phone," I say, the words hardly sounding real. "They saw my story online and want to make a film out of it. They've got Samuel L Jackson in mind to star in it. They want to pay me a lot of money, probably a six figure sum they said!"

"My God..." Her jaw drops. "You better not be kidding me here."

"No Mum, seriously." She must be able to tell by my face; it feels as if my muscles have turned to custard.

"Honestly?" Mum says her eyes widening in excitement.

"Yes, honestly!"

Mum's grin spreads across her face.

"They did specify one condition though," I smile. "I have to write a sequel."

*

Zombies on a Boat part 2: Attack of the Vampires

And it went dark and the humans were all dead and the zombies and quokkas ate what was left of the humans and there was guts and shit everywhere and the zombies loved it and rolled round in it and the quokkas fucked in it cuz that's what they do all the time. Then suddenly a vampire walked in with jet black hair and a sweeppy fringe holding some hair straighteners. He had like fangs and like orange-y coloured eyes and pale skin and all that usual vampire crap. He looked at the zombies who all turned and gasped at exactly the same time and the quokkas even stopped fucking for a moment to look at him. The zombies all jumped on him and started to try and eat him but he was like "duh, I'm undead, you can't eat me, you stupid lame zombies'

He flicked his fringe and went off to get his vampire mates, who also all had sweeppy fringes but hadn't heard any of the comottion cuz they had been busy straightnin their hair. They all went to find the PA system to go and put their Emo music on. The zombies hated it and hid at the other end of the ferry and the quokkas hated it even more and their brains exploaded, and then the zombies ate the quokkas brains.

The vampires had a human girl with them with some weird reason who they called Ella and they took it in turns to have sex with her and she loved it. Then suddenly a warewolf came along but he was still in human form, but they knew he was a warewolf cuz his jeans were all ripped up and he had no T-shirt on and was rediculousely muscley and tanned.

"Oh Drake!" the slutty human girl said and ran over to him and pulled down his jeans and started sucking him off. The main vampire guy (by the way his name is Edwin) started fucking her in the arse at the same time

whilst Paramore played through the PA. But the zombies had now seen the girl and started trying to eat her until Drake finally actually turned into a werewolf and ripped their heads off with his big teeth. But it was too late cuz the girl had already been bit by a zombie and so started turning into a zombie, but Drake didn't relaise she was turning into a zombie and started trying to put his furry dog cock in her zombie mouth but she bit it off and spat it at Edwin who was all stropy cuz it messed up his hair.

Then the warewolves killed the rest of the vampires and the zombies.

Finally they could do the one thing they had actually come to do in the first place…………………….turn off the awful music.

The End!!

~

Mel Ciavucco's Biography

Mel Ciavucco is a Bristol based writer, originally from Staffordshire. Her short stories have been published in the *Sentinel Literary Quarterly* magazine and in the *Darker Times* fiction anthology. She was a Notable Contender for the *Bristol Short Story Prize*, and won third place in the *Henshaw Press* short story contest. She is currently working on a screenplay for her first feature film, plus a short film, plus finishing her novel *Occasus* which is a post-apocalyptic drama. In amongst all this she works for a counselling charity and in the very little spare time she has left she enjoys cooking, yoga and going to the cinema, but not all at the same time.

Mel's website: www.melciavucco.weebly.com

~

Mel's Competition Judging Comments

I have an apology to make to all the unknown judges I've secretly cursed after not winning various competitions! Now I understand how hard it is to be a judge – there are so many talented writers out there (and funny too!). This was very, very hard. If I had my way I'd of picked about six stories for the number-one spot. Well done to everyone who was shortlisted, you've all brought a smile to my face. It really is an honour to be a judge, so thanks again to all the writers and to Chris Fielden for making all this possible.

A FINAL NOTE

Thank you to everyone who has purchased this anthology. I hope you have enjoyed reading it as much as I have enjoyed putting it together.

Until next year!

Chris Fielden

Made in the USA
Charleston, SC
07 November 2014